Merry
Christmas,
Madku ♥

May the
banner over 2018
be Faith,
Hope +
Love

Michele

21 Days of Hope

A Daily Encounter

21 Days of Hope

A Daily Encounter

David Crone

Dedication

This book is dedicated to my family.
Each of you have a unique place in my heart.

Acknowledgement

I wish to thank those who made this book possible: Nathanael White for helping to give this book a target; my personal assistant, Lila Hunt, for her collaboration in developing the activations; Dan McCollam, who always challenges me to be more than I think I am; and my wife, Deborah, for her encouragement, ideas, and patience.

Endorsements

I have known David and Deborah Crone for over 20 years. I have watched David walk through the pain of the sudden death of his adult daughter, leaving him and Deborah with two young grandchildren to raise. In the midst of this unfathomable heartbreak, David emerged with the keys of hope for the world. In this new book, "21 Days of Hope," David releases an impartation for a lifestyle of hope that is built on his own testimony and the beautiful process out of discouragement. This is more than a daily devotional; this is a powerful roadmap for a lifestyle dominated by the joyful expectation of God's good works. This book will deliver you from the prison of hopelessness and help launch you into your divine destiny! I highly recommend this book to anyone who isn't yet living in the fullness of what it means to be a hope-filled believer, and I know that the timing of its release is crucial to this moment in history!

Kris Vallotton
Leader, Bethel Church, Redding, CA
Co-Founder of Bethel School of Supernatural Ministry
Author of eleven books, including The Supernatural Ways of Royalty, Heavy Rain and Destined to Win.

This book is a River of hope, a weapon against the discouraging fixations of life. 21 Days of Hope is a stream of emotional, mental and spiritual armor and you will find yourself wanting to read everyday in one day! Your wings of hope will spread with each day of reading and meditation, and comfort will become a wall around your heart and soul.

Ivan Tait, Author of Letters From God

Foreword

To have a friend who is a prisoner of hope is a rare and precious treasure. I first met David Crone more than twenty-five years ago when we served together on the staff of a large church. He was already widely known for his impeccable character and integrity, but that alone is not what sets him apart from others. In vocational ministry circles, it's not uncommon to meet champions who build great and impressive ministries through their faith. You also find an admirable number of ministers who serve broken humanity with measures of love and compassion. In my experience, it is men of abundant hope that are the rare exception.

Through the years I've watched David and his wife, Deborah, stare down giants of adversities while holding on unshakably to hope. Even in the darkest of circumstances, their hope rooted in faith and grounded in love could not be quenched. I have found David Crone to be a true prisoner of hope. One of the many benefits of walking with someone captivated by hope is that it is impossible to stay discouraged in their presence. Walking with one of hope's heroes keeps you in a healthy place of constantly expecting to see the goodness of God in the land of the living. This has been my pleasure in doing life with a friend like David Crone.

Concerning this journal, I've read that it takes 21 days to make or break any habit. In this 21-day journal David invites us into hope's gymnasium. He builds our hope muscles through inspirational and transformational thoughts. He crafts prayers over us that release impartations of the many manifold flavors of hope. David reintroduces us to the God of all hope so that we can overflow with hope by the power of the Holy Spirit.

It is my prayer that walking with David on this 21-day journey will press you into the safety and security of Jesus, the fortress of hope. I desire that any thought under the power of hopelessness would be radically and eternally over thrown by the goodness of God. I pray that you would emerge and arise utterly healed of any heart sickness caused by a hope deferred. I believe that 21 Days of Hope will craft an army of hope's heroes and champions who will restore this rare treasure in the earth. May God bless your journey.

Dan McCollam

International Director of Sounds of the Nations and author of books including, "The Prophetic Company."

Contents

Introduction

My captivation with the expectation of good was birthed out of a personal tragedy. The journey following that life-altering event led me to write the book *Prisoner of Hope: Captivated by the Expectation of Good.* I have been pleased with the reception the book has had around the world and thankful for its impact on those who have embraced its message. However, upon releasing that book, I began to recognize that as my good friend and colleague Dan McCollam says, the key to breakthrough is follow-through. God offers us an over-the-top experience in hope that can only be ours when the expectation of good becomes a lifestyle.

The Amplified Version of Romans 15:13 gives us the assurance of the more God offers: *May the God of your hope so fill you with all joy and peace in believing—through the experience of your faith-that by the power of the Holy Spirit you may abound and be overflowing—bubbling over—with hope.*

A few years ago, I became fascinated by the following thought spoken by a character in a reality show I was watching: *What you don't fully embrace, you trivialize.* It so stunned me that I rewound the scene and listened to it several times. I have since come to understand the real power of those words and added this to it: What you trivialize, you never fully possess.

There are many territories opened to us by a generous and good God that we have been invited to possess. There are the territories of our prophetic words, biblical promises, geographical locations, relationships, and atmospheres to name a few. One of those territories we can enter and possess is the territory of hope.

I believe the concept of hope has been trivialized and underestimated by misuse, overuse, and a lack of understanding of its importance to our lives. It's time to fully embrace hopeful expectation, possess its territory and allow it to confront the massive attack on hope we are seeing in our nation and around the world.

Unless we choose hope, activate our will, and go on a journey with the Holy Spirit, we will fail to gain the territory God offers us, found in a lifestyle dominated and overflowing with the expectation of good.

Joshua's instruction to the people of Israel as they prepared to go into the promised land was direct and straight forward: *Prepare provisions for yourselves, for within three days you will cross over this Jordan, to go in to possess the land which the Lord your God is giving you to possess.* Joshua 1:11. Notice, they were to go in, and they were to possess.

There is a difference between going in and possessing. The nation of Israel entered the land; however, if you compare a map of the territory God promised them and the territory they actually possessed, you will find a large discrepancy. They entered but they didn't possess the land.

To possess is to seize, dispossess, and occupy. To seize is to take hold of intentionally and aggressively—to grab as if what you're seizing belongs to you. There is no half-hearted, tentative effort when seizing to possess.

To dispossess is to face and defeat the resistors that will always be on the land that belongs to you. A friend of mine once stated, "The giant that is in front of you is standing on territory that belongs to you." If you don't dispossess the resisters, the resisters will do what they do best—resist—and you will lose the ground you have seized.

To occupy is to establish a lasting presence. It is to live from, take responsibility for, and build on the territory you have seized. The new territory becomes the context for your life.

Possessing an abundant, overflowing, bubbling-up kind of hope requires seizing it with tenacity, destroying the resisters in our expectation, and choosing to live every day in the context of hope.

When our 31-year-old daughter died suddenly, leaving us with two young grandchildren, we had a number of choices thrust on us. One of the most important choices had to do with our expectations for the future. We had to choose whether to live in sadness, emptiness, and grief, or possess the territory of hope.

The journey has not always been comfortable and there have been many tears along the way. But when we chose to live in the expectation of good from a good God, hope became more than a concept; it became our constant companion and a lifestyle.

You may wonder why 21 days of hope? In my experience when desiring transformational breakthrough, 21-day periods have been especially effective. I have found this to be true when fasting for greater intimacy with God, when resetting my physical metabolism, and when establishing a lifestyle habit.

I encourage you to return to *21 Days of Hope* on an annual basis for a hope check-up. No matter where you are in your journey, this book will help you possess fresh new territories of expectation.

21 Days of Hope is more than a book you read. It is designed to take you on a journey: a journey that will move you from ineffective wishing to empowered hoping, and a journey that will release you from being held hostage to circumstances so you can become a joyful prisoner of hope.

Angel Ladd, one of the worship leaders at The Mission in Vacaville, Ca. composed the following song after hearing me address the subject of hope. Her words beautifully capture the main thoughts found in this book.

I'm captivated
By this expectation
That all things work for my good
No price can stop me
From the prize set before me
Nothing can keep me from you.

I'm choosing hope
I'm choosing life
Fill me with joy, here in your presence
I'm choosing hope I'm choosing life
Fill me with joy, here in your presence.

From "Choosing Hope" by Angel Ladd
Used by permission

How to get the most out of 21 Days of Hope

This book is designed to be experienced over a 21-day period. However, since this book is to be approached in partnership with the Holy Spirit, feel free to journey at His pace.

Although you will discover your own approach to this book, there are elements in its design with specific purpose. Participating in each of the following sections is important for you to receive the book's full value in your hope adventure:

Hope Thought: This section gives you a brief Biblical study in hope to read and explore each day. You will be challenged in any negative or restrictive mindset and be encouraged into higher levels of engagement with hope. Every day's thought will start or end your day with the expectation of good.

Hope Activation: Every day's contemplation has suggested activations that will assist you in possessing hope. These activations are the key to moving from enjoying a "good thought," to experiencing transformation.

Hope Meditation: Additional Biblical references are suggested for every day's study. These are there for you to meditate on in partnership with Holy Spirit and gain further revelation. You will find space available for you to journal your discoveries.

Hope Prayer: The prayer at the end of each day's thought is a suggested starting place for you to have a conversation with God. I encourage you to craft your own personal expressions and declarations. Always remember that every time you pray, something happens.

What about small-group study?

21 Days of Hope is easily used for a small-group experience. Taking one or two days of hope each week, the group leader can encourage dialogue on the day's thought, the individual's experience in the activations, and revelations gained from their Bible meditations. In this way, with the addition of the participants praying for each other, small groups should experience both hopeful expectation and healthy community.

Ephesians 1:18

"I pray that the eyes of your heart may be enlightened, so that you will know what is the hope of His calling, what are the riches of the glory of His inheritance in the saints."

nasb

Day 1

Hope's Calling

*P*aul, in his letter to the Ephesian Christians, is praying that we will see, in order to understand. The old adage, "seeing is believing" has merit in that our eye gate is one of the most powerful ways that we come to understand, accept, or value a thing.

In the early 1970's there was a big push among environmentalist to save the humpback whale. There was a concern that they were being overharvested, and if that continued, they would become extinct. At the same time, the nation was beginning to accept abortion as not only legal but also a matter of choice that was moral.

I didn't get it. It didn't make sense to me that people could be so passionate about saving the whale while caring little if at all for the death of a child in the womb. The whale is just an animal was my contention, and a fetus is a human being. What was so great about humpback whales?

A few years later, Deborah and I traveled to Maui, Hawaii, and secured a beachfront condo for a holiday. It was only a dozen or so yards from our lanai to the edge of the water, and the view was stunning. It was whaling season, a time when the humpback whales arrived to the waters around Hawaii and gave birth to their calves. We had been to the islands before but never during whale season.

After settling into the condo, we walked out to the edge of the beach and gazed at the ocean passage between Maui and the island of Molokai. It was then that a large humpback breached not far off shore. It was a stunning show of power, strength and beauty. I stood captivated by what I had seen and in that moment, my response was an excited question, *Deb, did you see that?* Followed by a passionate declaration, *We have to save these whales!*

What happened? I saw, and I then understood. It didn't reduce my love for the unborn, but it did increase my value for the humpback whales, and I understood the passion of those wanting to save them.

So, what is it that Paul wants us to see so we can understand? It is the hope of God's calling. Paul wants us to grasp the enormity of the hope that God has called us into. In other words, we have been called—invited—into a hope that can only be fully understood when we see it through the eyes of our inner man.

There is great power in an invitation. When invited into something or somewhere, you are being granted access to see, experience, or somehow participate in a way you could not if not for the invitation.

An invitation declares value for the one being invited. Can you remember how it felt when someone you cared for invited you out to dinner? It said to you that you were valued enough by this person to be included in his or her life." In accepting that invitation, you were granted access into a personal part of his life and gained further understanding of who he was.

Several years ago, Deborah and I spoke at a prayer conference in London, England, with our dear friends, Rod and Julie Anderson, who have a powerful prayer ministry with members of Parliament. Because of their influence, we were invited to have tea with Lord Taylor in the House of Lords tea room that is only accessible by invitation. We had tea and scones with our friends and a Lord in a room that we could never have otherwise entered if not for an invitation.

Now, here is what Paul wants us to see so we can understand: we have been invited by the Lord of Lords to experience a hope that can only be comprehended by those who respond to His invitation. That, fellow prisoner of hope, is you and me.

What is this hope? It is the hope of our salvation-—being forgiven, set free, and no longer under condemnation. It is the hope that gives us confidence that we can stand before God without shame, being fully accepted and valued. It is the hope of our inheritance as a much-loved child.

What is this hope? It is the hope that for the rest of our lives here on earth we will be kept in Him; that every time we pray He hears us; that when we ask for wisdom we will receive it; that we will experience all he promised; and that our lives are built on a rock that will last forever.

What is this hope? It is all of the above and heaven, too. It is the hope of resurrection power and eternal life. It is the hope of being restored to loved ones gone before us. It is the hope of treasure kept for us in heaven, where nothing can destroy or steal it.

What is this hope? It's not a what; it is a person, and His name is Jesus, the hope of glory. It is into an intimate life with Him that we have been invited to possess.

Paul completes his prayer by asking that we would see in order to grasp the *riches of the glory of his inheritance in the saints.* Simply said, Paul is praying that we will discover and fully experience just how valuable we are to God. You and I are His treasure, His pearl of great price, and His valued possession.

We have been invited to explore the far reaches of His majesty and splendor, to go on an adventure with Him in His Kingdom as prisoners of hope, absolutely captivated by all the good He has prepared for us in this world and the next.

Activation:

1. Pray Paul's prayer from Ephesians 1:18 over yourself at least five times today. Also, pray this prayer for friends or loved ones that have lost hope.
2. Think of the last time you recognized that God was inviting you into an adventure with Him. Has the excitement of that encounter worn off? Choose today to hope and believe that Jesus is still extending an invitation to you, ready to dance with you into the next adventure. Ask Him to show you what He is inviting you into today and journal about His response. Remember, to accept His invitation only takes a simple yes.

Meditation:

Ephesians 1,2

Prayer:

Dear Father,

thank you that by inviting me to be in your Son, Jesus, you have placed a value on me that I could never comprehend. I accept your invitation to put my hope in you and experience all the wonders and joys you plan for me to receive. I choose to live in partnership with you with delightful expectation of a lifelong and eternal journey.

Journal

Zach 9:12

"Return to the stronghold, you prisoners of hope. Even today I declare, that I will restore double to you."

nkjv

Day 2

Hope's Captivation

*H*ave you ever been captivated by a thought, an image, or a possibility? Of course, you have. You may not be aware of it, but even now you are captivated by something. That something has your attention even when you are not consciously aware of it. It is like a program on your computer that is always running in the background.

In dealing with the nation of Israel through 70 years of captivity in Babylon, God offered them a choice in their captivation. They could either be captured by their circumstances, or captivated by hope. God even offered them a new identity as prisoners of hope. They could take on their new identity as a people captivated by the expectation of good or remain in their adopted identity as a people imprisoned in their present situation. He gives you and me the same choice.

What captivates you identifies you and will define the path into your future. Your expectations for this day and how you see yourself will in part be predicated on what you choose to be captivated by.

In Psalms 137 we have a clear depiction of what Israel chose as their captivation and adopted as their identity in the early years of life in Babylon:

By the rivers of Babylon, there we sat down, yea, we wept, when we remembered Zion.

Those who this picture depicts were fixated on what they had lost and the condition they were presently in. They saw only a past possessed with regret, a present filled with few choices, and a future owned by their captors. Hope was under attack.

Their captivation determined their actions, *We hung our harps upon the willows in the midst of it.*

What a tragic verse of hopelessness. The harps represented their national song, their hopes, and their redemptive message. It is my contention that the last thing they should have done is to hang their harps on the willows and refuse to use them to declare the message of hope, not only to themselves but also to the nation of their new home.

The nation of Israel was chosen by God to represent or re-present Him to other nations and people. The children of Israel were carriers of divine revelation and people of God's favor. They had a history replete with stories that contained signs, wonders, and miracles. They experienced and understood the power of redemption. And even though their rebellion led to their captivity, they still possessed the song of the God of hope.

That song should have been sung in a way that would cause jealousy among the nations. What better place to tune the harp and sing of hope than in a foreign land? If there was any nation that needed a revelation of God, it was Babylon, and these Jews carried that revelation. It was God's ultimate purpose to reveal Himself through the children of Israel. It was His hope that this revelation would be for the purpose of blessing those nations. If anything, they should have tuned their harps, not hung them on a tree.

Israel had the opportunity of a lifetime to be a transformational agent for a nation in need of God. Instead, they were captivated by their circumstances, hung their harps on the willow, and gave up their true identity. Ultimately, they devalued their legacy. Instead of living as prisoners of hope, they silenced their voice and headed down the road to a 70-year experience in a waterless pit.

Now near the end of their captivity, God through the prophet Zachariah is reminding Israel of their true identity and giving them the opportunity to choose their captivity thereby determining their identity

Return to the stronghold, you prisoners of hope. Even today I declare, that I will restore double to you. Zechariah 9:12

What is captivating you right now? What fascinates you to the point that it is determining your attitudes, your emotions, or your expectations? Today may not look like it's going to be the day you wanted it to be. You may not have the choice to change or alter your external circumstances. However, you can choose to have an internal fascination with hope, an expectation of good that will transform your perspective, increase your prospects, and cause you to live in your true identity.

Here is good news for you, who are reading this hope thought: God is offering you a choice. You can choose your captivation, thereby choosing your future. Choosing to be a prisoner of hope is to rest your future upon a God whose goodness is aimed at you. It is to live with good as your expectation and not the negative possibilities of your life situation. It is to live in your true identity. You are a prisoner of hope.

Regardless of the season you are in right now, this is God's call to you: Become a prisoner of hope. Embrace hope. Breathe hope. Meditate on hope. Soak in hope. Plant yourself in hope. Take hope as a core element of your identity.

Activation:

1. Write down what is captivating your attention today. Ask Holy Spirit to show you hope in the midst of these circumstances.
2. Write a declaration of your intent to be captivated by hopeful

   expectation and read it out loud at least 7 times today.

Meditation:

Philippians 4:8

Colossians 3:2

Prayer:

Father,

thank you for all you have offered to me as your child. Thank you that I don't have to live under the situations that are in front of me, but I can be fascinated with you and the hope you offer. I praise you for captivating my heart and allowing me to expect good today.

Journal

Zach 9:11

I will set your prisoners free from the waterless pit.

nkjv

Day 3

Hope's Release

Not all of life is filled with sunshine, roses, and ice cream sundaes. I'm not at all suggesting that it's all bad, but we know that some of it is like the *waterless pit* identified here in Zachariah. There are days even months, and for some, years that can feel dry and lacking in refreshing. These times or seasons are often brought on by crises or tragic circumstances.

Hope is a personal subject to my wife and me. It's not business, it's personal, and it's not theory. It's a living reality we embraced out of desperation as we endured some of the worst life can throw at a person. Faced with the sudden death of our 31-year-old daughter and a mother of two young children, we stood at the brink of a pit experience.

The darkest day following Amy's death came the day when Samuel, her 18-month-old son, realized mom was no longer with him. Deborah had carried him into the kitchen where he, his sister, and his mom ate breakfast every morning. He took one look at the place where his mom always sat and somehow knew that life had taken a terrible turn.

I will never forget the agony and pain expressed in his weeping and the horrifying feeling of helplessness that swept over Deborah and me. No matter what we said or did, we could not comfort him. We were trapped in a waterless pit with seemingly no way of escape. And then the phone rang, and hope marched into the room.

Deborah answered the phone to find one of our dear friends, Carol Dew, on the other end of the line. Through tears of agony Deborah poured out her heart to Carol. Carol responded by giving us a lesson in hope. She reminded Deborah, *You know what to do; I've seen you do this before.* She then instructed Deb to take Samuel to his bed and speak to him calmly and confidently, addressing his spirit. *Tell him*, she said, *it's going to be ok, that grandma and papa are right here, and you, Samuel, are going to be alright.*

Deb followed Carol's instructions and began to speak words of hope. *Samuel, your mommy is in heaven now, and we will miss her. But you don't need to be afraid. We will take care of you, and you will be alright.* As she continued to speak, Samuel melted in her arms and listened. As Deb finished, he jumped into his crib, lay down, and went to sleep. From that day on Samuel was a contented and happy little child, and he never again repeated that first day's experience in any form. Hope had swept him and us out of the waterless pit and into a stronghold of hopeful expectation.

David, the boy who would be king, had many times in his journey from shepherd to ruler that must have felt like living in a waterless pit. He often found himself in desperate situations that held little to no hope in the natural. His experience in Ziklag was one of those times.

David and his men had been out raiding the enemies of Israel and were returning to their families in Ziklag. When they arrived, they found that the Amalikites had taken everything and everyone. All their children, wives, and everything of value had been carried off in their absence. The Bible records that David and his men cried until they had no more tears to cry.

It only got worse for David as his men turned on him and threatened to kill him. He was in a waterless pit of hopeless circumstances. It was in that moment that David stirred himself up and strengthened himself in the Lord. He turned to the God of hope and found the answer for his desperate dilemma. The result was that David recovered all that had been taken and more.

Perhaps you are facing a day or living in a season like we were or like David did. You are desperate for hope that your life will change for the better but lacking any outward sign that it will. Maybe that isn't you and instead, maybe you're in a season of rich blessing, but you still know God has more for you. Either way, I can tell you from experience that there is no wrong time to cultivate strongholds of hope in your soul.

In seasons of abundance, we cultivate hope to ward off complacency and apathy, regarding the blessing God calls us to become. Meanwhile, in times seemingly bereft of hope, we must hope even more. On our worst day—his hope can be our deliverer.

The waterless pit is not the place intended by God for us to live. His provision for our dwelling is a place filled with joy, peace, and contentment. It's called His presence, and it is where prisoners of hope have access 24/7.

Activation:

1. Write down everything in your current situation that looks hopeless. These form your *waterless pit.* Thank God in prayer that He is removing you from this pit.
2. Ask God to speak His promises over your situation. These form your prison of hope. Declare to the Lord your choice to live only in this prison of hope.

Meditation:

I Samuel 30:1-20

Psalms 16:11

Psalms 91:1-2

Prayer:

Lord Jesus,

you are the Captain and Author of my hope. No circumstance is hopeless to you. Even when you were dead, you came back alive! I declare over my circumstances that you are stronger than anything that comes against me, and you are more determined for my good than my enemies are for my harm. I choose to look at your promises today instead of my circumstances. I determine that I will leave my waterless pit and make myself a prisoner of hope

Journal

Zach 9:12

Return to the stronghold, you prisoners of hope...

nkjv

Day 4

Hope's Stronghold

S trongholds are welcomed or unwelcomed, depending on your perspective. If you're on the outside looking in, they can be intimidating and formidable. If you are taking refuge in one, they are comforting and protective.

Picture yourself outside, exposed to the freezing conditions of a winter in the state of Minnesota, considered one of the coldest states in the United States. You are not properly dressed for that kind of weather; you have not had adequate sleep in days; and your last meal was yesterday. You are cold, hungry, and exhausted.

Now imagine that you are standing in front of a large, beautiful, and welcoming home. You can see through the window that there is food on the table, a roaring fire in the fireplace, and you know that everything you need for your survival and protection from the elements are behind those walls and through the large door. However, there is an imposing lock on that door and a sign that reads, *No Entry*.

That house for you is either a stronghold of protection and provision or it is a stronghold of frustration and resistance. The factor that will determine if you die in the snow or thrive in the house is access. Do you have the key to the lock, and do you have permission to enter?

Walking through Warwick castle more than a decade ago, I was impressed by both its history and its function. It was built in the year 1068 by William the Conqueror and used as a stronghold until the early 17th century. It was then turned into a retreat for the nobility and royalty, hosting parties for the rich and famous. Today it is a fascinating museum, displaying its once distinguished history.

In its best days, Warwick castle was a small city with shops and manufacturing. Anything needed for living in that day could be found or constructed inside the walls. Weapons necessary for defensive or offensive warfare were produced in the castle's foundry. Cloth was woven and clothing manufactured along with utensils for cooking. It not only provided protection and provision for those living within its walls, it was a stronghold that those living outside the walls would run to in times of enemy attack and come into for necessary provision.

In all its history, the walls of Warwick Castle were never breached or overrun by an enemy. That is an impressive statistic when you consider the many invaders in English history. Warwick was an impenetrable stronghold. To its enemies, it was a stronghold of resistance; to its occupants, it was a stronghold of safety. For those who had access through its gate, it was a stronghold of hope.

The strength and function of Warwick Castle is not far removed in type to the one referred to in Zachariah's prophecy as "The Stronghold." The prophet was giving the Jews permission to re-enter a stronghold that they had deserted. In type, that was the city of Jerusalem. However, the prophecy here is referring to a person not a building.

David makes reference to this stronghold when he writes, *The Lord is my rock and my fortress and my deliverer; My God, my strength, in whom I will trust; my shield and the horn of my salvation, my stronghold.* (Psalms 18:2)."

The stronghold for the prisoner of hope is none other than God himself. In Him is all the provision and security you need. And here is the good news on this day of hope—you have access. You have permission to come out of the cold. As a child of God, you not only have permission to run into Him in the day of need, but to be resident in His presence 24/7.

I normally travel an average of 100,000 miles on airplanes each year. One thing I learned very quickly is the concept of access. More often than not when planning my travel, I purchase the least expensive ticket available and can anticipate a common experience when boarding the plane.

I enter the plane and walk through or can see first class. Every passenger has a separate pod that becomes a bed and experiences a level of service comparable to a 5 star hotel and restaurant. I can see it, but I can't have it because I don't have the ticket that gives me access.

I then walk through the business class section with extra wide seats, extended legroom, and seats that lay flat for sleeping. It is very similar to the first-class section but not the same level of comfort or service. Again, I can see it, but I can't have it. My ticket reads, *economy class.*

One of the sweetest words in the English language to the frequent flyer is *upgrade*. Upgrade means we have access to something greater. When we entered the Kingdom of God through Jesus Christ, we received the greatest upgrade in the universe—an upgrade into the stronghold of his presence.

Living in God's presence is the most natural place for you to reside. His presence is your authentic stronghold. From the moment God formed man from the dust of the earth and breathed the breath of life into him, the human race was designed to experience all of its existence in relationship with and in constant communion with God. When He formed you in your mother's womb and knit your inner parts together with His own hands, you were destined to live in Him.

Living in the presence is not only our natural habitat, it is the privilege of every believer. Everywhere He is, everything He is, is present and available to us. However, living from that reality is still a choice that we are responsible for every day.

Activation:

1. Visualize yourself being welcomed into a house where there is everything you need. What would you find there? Choose today to step into your rightful home in God's presence and ask Him to show you how to access whatever you need.
2. Consider how you have seen yourself in relationship to whatever resistance you're facing. Ask the Holy Spirit to guide you into the hope-filled stronghold of God's presence and to see yourself and your resistance the way He sees it.
3. Set a reminder on your phone for every hour today, and take a moment to choose the stronghold of hope, knowing that God's presence is with and all around you.

Meditation:

Psalm 16:11   Colossians 2:9-10   Ephesians 2

Prayer:

Thank you Father that you have purchased my access into the stronghold of your presence by the sacrifice of your Son, Jesus. I denounce all other strongholds that I have relied on, and I run into you as my strong tower, my stronghold, and my true hope.

Journal

Zach 9:11

Because of the blood of your covenant I will set your prisoners free

nkjv

Day 5

Hope's Covenant

*P*romises, promises! If there is one thing I've learned in my years of working with people, it's that promises made are only as good as the character of the person making them. Character demonstrated is the only real collateral that means anything.

When Deborah and I were just a few years married, we explored the possibility of building a home. I had a small insurance settlement that would provide the majority of the funds, so we began to look for a builder and property. We secured a building lot and contracted with a man I only now remember as Gino. We gave him a down payment and waited for the project to begin. Several weeks went by with no work being accomplished, and we lost contact with Gino.

Eventually, we were notified by the Sheriff's department that Gino was a confidence man that left the county with hundreds of thousands of dollars of other people's money, ours included. We were devastated and wept with useless contract in hand. Promises, promises.

Through the prophet Zachariah, God promises to rescue the people of Israel from their waterless pit. This would certainly be a welcomed promise to those Jews still being held in captivity for over seventy years. For many of them their homeland was only a distant memory, and freedom a painful longing. For the others who were born and raised in Babylon, they knew nothing of freedom and their homeland was in their imagination, pictures painted by the stories they heard as children.

This was a welcomed promise indeed. But can they believe it? Dare they hope that what God is promising will come to pass?

God didn't leave them without a reason for embracing hope in His promises and declares through the prophet, *Because of the blood of your covenant, I will set your prisoners free.* God was reminding the Jews of both His nature as a covenant-keeping God and of a specific covenant with Moses, recorded in Exodus 23 and sealed with a sacrifice in Exodus 24.

In Chapter 23:20-33 God speaks to Moses, reminding the people of His promise to give Israel the land and Israel's responsibility to make no other covenants with those in the land. This territory spoken of in Exodus is the same land that the Jews now coming from captivity were to occupy. Then in Chapter 24 Moses records the covenant in a book, and we read the following:

Then he (Moses) *took the Book of the Covenant and read in the hearing of the people... and Moses took the blood, sprinkled it on the people and said, 'This is the blood of the covenant which the Lord has made with you according to all these words.*

God's covenant-keeping nature and the specific covenant made with Moses, was the security for the promises now being made to those in the waterless pit of captivity.

It was foolish to place one's hope in the promises of someone like Gino, but here is the good news—God is no Gino. His promises are yes and amen, which simply means if He said it, it is as good as done. His covenant promises to us are written with the blood of his Son and stand true in the trustworthiness of His character.

God, through the prophet Isaiah, asked a question in response to Israel's lament that God had forgotten them, *Can a woman forget her nursing child, and not have compassion on the son of her womb?* Isa 49:15

Most of us, because we could not imagine a mother deserting her child, would answer no to that question. God, having no such delusions, follows His question with a stunning reply and some powerful words of hope:

Surely they may forget. Yet, I will not forget you. See, I have inscribed you on the palms of my hands. Isaiah 49:15-16

He cannot forget you; He cannot fail to keep His promises to you. His very life was given to guarantee His faithfulness. You can place your hope in Him, for the nail holes in His hands are forever a reminder of His covenant with you.

Here is more good news: Not only did God seal our promises by the blood sacrifice of His Son, but He gave us Holy Spirit as a down payment to guarantee our inheritance.

And he has identified us as his own by placing the Holy Spirit in our hearts as the first installment that guarantees everything he has promised us. II Corinthians 1:22 NLT

A down payment is the assurance that everything else owed in a contract will be paid according to the details spelled out in the agreement. God has given us a down payment that cannot be excelled. He has guaranteed His word by giving us Himself.

Your hope is only as powerful as the one in whom you place your hope. Faithful is not just how God will always respond to you; it is who He is. He will not violate His own character. The placing of your hope is your choice and one that will reveal your level of trust and determine hope fulfilled or hope disappointed.

Activation:

1. Write down the important hopes you have and the one your hope is anchored in.
2. Ask God to show you the hopes that are placed in Him and those that may be misplaced. Seek His help in bringing those misplaced into alignment with Him.
3. Give Holy Spirit permission to give you courage throughout your day to abandon useless places of hope and embrace hope in Him.

Meditation:

II Corinthians 1:18-22

Ephesians 1:11-14

Hebrews 11:11

Prayer:

Father,

I place my trust in you today for you are the anchor of my hope. Thank you that you have proven your faithfulness to me, and I embrace the cross as my guarantee of your future fidelity. I welcome Holy Spirit's affirmation of my inheritance. I declare that your promises are "yes" to me, and I come into agreement with your amen with my amen.

Journal

Romans 4:18

Who, contrary to hope, in hope believed.

nkjv

Day 6

Hope's Choosing

*A*ll of us have negative circumstances that we may or may not have the power to change. They are real, and if left unchanged, have consequences. However, there are truths that are a greater level of reality when those truths reside in an eternal God who does not lie and is completely trustworthy.

An example of this is found in Jesus' words to His disciples, *In this world, you will have tribulation, but be of good cheer, for I have overcome the world*. John 16:33

There is no denying that there is trouble to be found in this journey on earth. It is a fact. However, the greater reality is the truth that Jesus has overcome that fact, and those who live in Him and choose to hope in Him are also overcomers.

Here is the good news: Living in hope is a choice that is available in every circumstance. Though we may not be able to change or alter our external situation, we can choose to have an internal hope that will transform our perspective and increase our prospects.

Abraham had every reason to accept his situation as hopeless. His history of decades of failure to produce a child through Sarah declared it would never happen. Sarah had always been barren, and there was no evidence that her condition was going to improve any time soon.

Their age at the time Paul is referring to in his letter to the Romans is nearly a hundred years old. This fact certainly did not bode well for their prospects. Every year that passed increased the pressure to give up hope. There was nothing in Abraham's life that gave evidence that the promise of God would come to pass—except—it was the promise of God. That promise was the truth that stood as Abraham's greater reality in the face of the facts. Abraham chose the truth and placed his hope in God.

To accept that our situation is hopeless is to abandon our professed belief that God is greater than our circumstance. Hope is living above the facts and choosing the truth of God's promises as our reality. The late Norman Cousins, American journalist, author, and professor, made a statement that mirrors this premise: *Hope is independent of the apparatus of logic.*

You can't reason your way into hope because hope at its very core is unreasonable. It must be chosen by an act of the will. Analysis, calculation, and human logic, if allowed dominance, will diminish your hope and cancel faith.

After the death of our daughter, I was struck with an aggressive bout of bronchitis that became resistant to any of the doctor's treatment. At best, all they could do was keep it from developing into pneumonia. This continuing physical struggle, added to the deep sorrow over the loss of Amy, left me wondering if this condition was a glimpse of my future. The more I focused on my circumstance the more I was bombarded by doubt and despondency.

The battle for hope came to a climax in the early morning hours, following a night of trying to breathe while caught in grief. As I sat with the Bible on my lap, Holy Spirit reminded me of the scripture targeted in this devotion and the words, *contrary to hope, in hope believed*, jumped off the pages and leapt into my spirit. I knew then that I had a choice; and with what little breath I could muster, I shouted, *I choose hope!*

I am happy to attest that my future has not been dominated by illness and unhealthy sorrow. My identity since that day has not been as a poor man that lost a daughter but the joyous man who is a carrier of hope.

Is there something—a circumstance, situation, or condition—standing in the way of the promise you hold in your heart? Does all your logic and human calculation say it can't be done? Do the facts predict your failure? Well, this is your day to step over the facts and into the greater reality of God's promises by choosing to live in hope.

The prophet Isaiah, in speaking to those who refused to give up even though their way of rebellion and spiritual adultery continued to be unrewarding, made this statement recorded in Isaiah 57:10: *You are wearied in the length of your way; yet you did not say, 'There is no hope.'* When I read this, I was challenged and forced to do a little personal check on my resolve to always choose hope.

I am not suggesting that we live a lifestyle contrary to our life in Christ. However, if those whose lifestyle gives them no evidence of advancement refuse to give up hope, how much more can we live tenaciously in the expectation of good?

We have the God of hope living in us and have every reason to live with the same resolve to never confess, *There is no hope*. In choosing to live in hope we are refusing to be victimized by our situation or helpless in our choices. We are not blind to the facts but our focus and our dependence is on the truth of God's promises as our superior reality.

Activation:

1. Be conscious of how much attention you are giving to the circumstances that would try to steal your hope today. Every time you hear yourself talk or think about the circumstances, stop and declare, *But I choose hope!* and thank Jesus for giving you an unfailing reason to hope.
2. Ask the Holy Spirit to lift any weight of despair off of you that has been brought on by facts. Take a few minutes to allow Him to encourage you and remind you of His greater reality.

Meditation:

Romans 5:13-22

Prayer:

Father,

thank you that your truth, your word, lives above the facts that I will face today. I choose to believe your word, declare it as my truth, and live in hope of a greater reality. I will not declare that there is no hope, but I will confess my hope in you in every situation and circumstance. Today, by your grace, I choose hope.

Journal

Philippians 3:13

I do not count myself to have apprehended; but one thing I do, forgetting those things which are behind and reaching forward to those things which are ahead...

nkjv

Day 7

Hope's Memory

Having a selective memory just may be a God-endorsed activity for prisoners of hope. It sure seems that Paul is encouraging, even modeling intentionally forgetting the things in the past that do not add to our advancement. He endorses this approach in Philippians 3:15, calling it the mindset of the mature and goes on to imply that to think otherwise is to have failed to receive God's truth on the subject.

Therefore let us, as many as are mature, have this mind; and if in anything you think otherwise, God will reveal even this to you.

Paul had much history to regret from when he was known as Saul. He was one who persecuted the followers of Jesus with absolute zeal. He traveled from city to city to identify and victimize any believer he found. It was on such a trip that he was knocked off his donkey and confronted with the truth that he was actually persecuting Christ himself: *Saul, Saul, why are you persecuting me? I am Jesus, the one you are persecuting.* Acts 9:4-5

Yet it is Paul who emphatically declares in what I hear in my imagination, spoken with a New York accent: Fuhgetaboutit!

The word Paul uses for forgetting means to give over to oblivion, to no longer give what is forgotten any place in one's life.

I like the New English Translation of Philippians 3:13, *I do not consider myself to have attained this. Instead I am single-minded: forgetting the things that are behind and reaching out for the things that are ahead...* Paul was single-minded in forgetting and in reaching with hope for what lay ahead. I believe it was his forgetting that allowed him to reach forward.

The apostle Peter like Paul had things to forget. He failed Jesus, the man he confessed to have loved and would never deny. I can't think of a larger failure than to deny knowing the one he had declared and believed to be the Christ, the Son of the living God.

It is interesting to me that Peter emphasizes hope so strongly in his writings. In the opening chapter of his first letter to Jewish believers, who were facing great persecution, Peter speaks of hope three times. In verse 3, he assures the believes that they were birthed into a vibrant, invigorating, life-producing hope through the resurrection of Jesus Christ; in verse 13, he encourages them to rest their hope on the grace that was given to them when Jesus was revealed to them; and in verse 21, he reminds them that their faith and their hope are in God.

Peter again emphasizes the importance of hope in 3:15, *...Always be ready to give a defense to everyone who asks you a reason for the hope that is in you, with meekness and fear.* For a man to fail so completely yet become the leader of the first century church and write so passionately about hope, Peter must have had a powerful forgetter.

Living in regret is a sure way to defeat our hope. Without dealing with the past, our hopeful expectation for today may be held hostage to our failures of yesterday, leaving us captive to shame and condemnation. Releasing those things that have been dealt with at the cross of Jesus and single-mindedly forgetting them—giving them over to oblivion—will set us free from their attachments and empower our hope for going after the good that is awaiting us.

Hope is established in truth that is believed and fully embraced. The facts may be telling you that you failed, but the truth of what Christ has accomplished on your behalf is the truth that sets you free. You see, it's not just about what we forget but the truth that we remember.

What is that truth?

The truth is this: You are a much-loved child of God. You are a new creation—not an improved version—but one of a different nature. You are the righteousness of God in Christ Jesus. You are His workmanship, created for good works. You are forgiven, redeemed, restored to the Father, and a joint heir with His Son. You are seated in heavenly places with Christ Jesus. You are a saint not a sinner, an adopted son not an orphan. You are a prisoner of hope.

It may be that you need to deal with a failure that requires forgiveness. Do it now, but come to God as His child not a beggar or a slave. Come with the expectation of one already accepted and loved not as a fatherless orphan.

When my oldest granddaughter was around three or four years of age, we were together in the church sanctuary. Following the morning service she decided to disobey me in a specific instruction I had given her. Her father saw the infraction and pulled her aside. Later that evening Samantha called our home phone and left a message on the recorder, a message I have the recording of to this day:

Papa, I'm sorry I disobeyed you. I love you. Good night.

You could hear in her voice that it was a heartfelt apology; but when done with her repentance, *I love you*. Good night was the light-hearted expression of a forgiven and free grandchild of her loving papa. She refused to live in a moment of regret or condemnation.

Today, prisoner of hope, *fuhgetaboutit!* and live free from the past, taking hold of the truth of what God has done for you and reach full-heartedly for the good He has reserved for this day.

Activation:

1. Ask Holy Spirit to reveal anything that has been forgiven and dealt with but which you still feel guilty about. Choose to forgive yourself and thank Him for His grace in which you can trust.
2. Declare the following truth aloud several times today: *I am a much-loved child of God. I am a new creation. I am the righteousness of God in Christ Jesus. I am his workmanship, created for good works. I am forgiven, redeemed, restored to my Father, and a joint heir with His Son. I am seated in heavenly places with Christ Jesus. I am a saint, not a sinner, an adopted son/daughter, not an orphan. I am a prisoner of hope!*

Meditation:

I John 1:5-2:2   Ephesians 1:3-12   Colossians 1:9-14

Prayer:

Father,

thank you that you have provided for me to live forgiven without shame or blame. I receive what you have made possible through your Son, Jesus, and forget those things that are behind me. I set my heart upon you and your truth; I set my focus on the good you have for me today, and I receive your grace to empower me to enjoy the blessings and endure with joy the trials.

Journal

Psalms 146:5

Happy is he who has the God of Jacob for his help, whose hope is in the Lord his God.

nkjv

Day 8

Hope's Anchor

Hope to be authentic and effective must be solidly anchored in something or someone that is trustworthy. Unattached hope or hope placed in temporal, vain, ineffective, or corrupted things is not hope at all but a wish. Psalms 33:17 refers to this kind of hope as vain or false hope.

A horse is a vain hope for safety; neither shall it deliver any by great strength.

We have all learned the lesson of misplaced hope and faith. It's no wonder that much of our population is jaded and lives with a level of hopelessness. The government has not been a bastion of hope; financial security has not been secure at all; and employers have scrambled to survive and cannot be the holder of our hope. Hope in our personal resources, our gifts, or our reputation is certainly unstable and fleeting.

Here's some important information for those of us who are prisoners of hope: These significant but often impotent parts of our world were never meant to be our anchor of hope and certainly not to be what we trust in to fulfill our hope. Here is the good news:

We have been offered the God of hope in whom we can put our trust and in whom we can find fulfillment. Hope, anchored in Him, is guaranteed by His character and nature and empowered by the Holy Spirit who lives in us.

There is a difference between hope *for* and hope *in*. I have many things I hope for—the future, my children's success, the growth and effectiveness of the ministry of the church I serve, and my personal development in God among others. All of this hoping *for* is healthy and sets our reticular activator – the part of our brain that sets our focus - to resist negativity. However, it only has meaning in relation to whom or what I place my hope in. Misplaced hope *in* will leave us shipwrecked on the rocks of circumstances that attempt to destroy our hope for.

Allow me a personal illustration: My daughter, Amy, had just experienced a hurtful and difficult time in her life. She had been betrayed by someone she loved and now faced a future with two little children to raise as a single mom. As a father, I was very proud of her tenacity, courage, and determination to move on and build a happy and healthy home for her and her children. I also had great hope for her future.

Then everything about her future on this earth changed in a moment when she collapsed into Deborah's arms and fell to our garage floor, and she was gone. To say it was devastating seems trite. It was the worst day of my life. Had my hope for her and her future with her family been in her strength and resolve or even in my ability as her father to help her establish her future, I don't believe I would have survived the tragedy of her death and remained healthy in any way. But my hope *for* was anchored in one who never changes in character or nature, on whose promises I can bank my life and the life of my children.

Deborah and I determined many years ago that we would live with a positive hope *for* approach to life. We also determined that our hope for our family and ministry would be anchored to our hope in God and His promises. We had settled the issues of the goodness of God. We had become resolute in the truth that His love for us is deep enough to reach down to our deepest pain and high enough to lift us into His arms of compassion and comfort. We lived confident in the promise of God that all things work together for our good.

So, when we left the body of our daughter in the hospital, our hope *for* was shattered; but our hope *in* held us through the pain. Because of the One we hope in, we have not been shipwrecked by the loss of our daughter, and our identity is not held captive by our grief. We will miss her till the day we see her in heaven—but we are not identified as the couple who lost a child, but as the people who are carriers of hope.

One more thought for this day of hope.

When Jesus told Peter, after he had fished all night and caught nothing, to go out into the deep part of the lake and fish. Peter's response tells us everything we need to know about his lack of hope for catching anything. *Master, we have toiled all night and caught nothing.* His hope *for* was virtually nonexistent. However, Peter didn't respond from his hope *for*, but from his hope in. *Nevertheless, at your word I will let down the net.* It was Peter's hope in the words of Jesus that motivated him to do what Jesus asked, and the result was a catch so large it required other boats to pull it in.

You may or may not have much hope for some of the things you will face today. Either way, live with a *Nevertheless* in your heart and respond out of your hope in the God of hope. Don't give up hoping for the things that are in your heart, but let your heart be settled in the goodness and love of the Father. As David declares,

Happy (Oh the Happiness, blessedness, joyfulness) is he who has the God of Jacob for his help, whose hope is in the Lord his God. Psalm 146:5, AMP

Activation:

1. Write down some things that you are hoping for. Offer them to the Lord and allow yourself to hope for them more thoughtfully this week.
2. Have a conversation with Holy Spirit about some delayed hopes in your life. Ask whether He wants to revive your hope *for* any of them based on His promises. Also, ask whether He wants to redirect your hope *in* any of them based on His nature. Finally, ask Him to comfort and redeem any other hopes that have been lost or destroyed.

Meditation:

Romans 15:13   Psalms 33:7   Psalms 42   Hebrews 6:19-20

Prayer:

Father,

thank you that you encourage me and give me permission to have dreams and to hope for good things in my life. You are good and desire good things for me. I declare that everything I hope for will be anchored in who you are and the promises you make. When what I hope for looks like it will not come to pass, I will say, 'Nevertheless, my hope is in you.'

Journal

Lamentations 3:21

Yet this I call to mind and therefore I have hope.

nkjv

Day 9

Hope's Thoughts

*H*ave you ever thought about what you're thinking about? Take a moment right now and think about what you are thinking about. Wow, there's a lot going on up there isn't there?

You may want to think about this: Your thoughts have more power than you may realize. Paul certainly understood this to be true when he wrote to the church in Philippi and gave them a list of things to think about:

Fix your thoughts on what is true, and honorable, and right, and pure, and lovely, and admirable. Think about things that are excellent and worthy of praise. Philippians 4:8, NIV

In his letter to the Romans, Paul states that our transformation into Godliness is linked to the way we think.

Do not be conformed to this world, but be transformed by the renewing of your mind. That you may prove what is that good and acceptable and perfect will of God. Romans 12:2,

He writes in his second letter to the Corinthians, emphasizing the responsibility we have to determine what we think by taking our thoughts captive so that we think like Christ:

We demolish arguments and every pretension that sets itself up against the knowledge of God, and we take captive every thought to make it obedient to Christ. II Corinthians 10:5, NIV

Your thoughts have the power to either encourage hope or dampen your expectation. What you think about can be a hope-thief or a hope-expander. Your thought life has the power to snatch expectation from the jaws of hope, or it can awaken hope in what seems to be a hopeless situation. The prophet Jeremiah was awakened to this reality as he was lamenting all his troubles.

In fact, the book of Lamentations—especially chapter 3—can be depressing until you get to verse 21 of that third chapter. Up to this point, all Jeremiah is thinking and writing about are all the discouraging, dispiriting, disappointing, and plain lousy things that have happened to him while he was trying to be a faithful prophet of God. He was persecuted by his own people, falsely accused of treason, and imprisoned for doing what God had told him to do. Jeremiah is called the weeping prophet for a reason and his book is well titled.

But then we come to the twenty-first verse and Jeremiah makes an about face in his thinking, and hope erupts: Yet, this I call to mind and therefore I have hope. In spite of all the things he had been through, Jeremiah declares that he will change what he's thinking about. In so doing, his hopelessness is replaced by the expectation of good.

Now, think about this: you can determine what you think about and how you think about what you think about. This means that what you think about and how you think about what you think about can actually determine the level of hope in your world. Wow—that's a lot of thinking!

One day I was thinking about my daughter and remembering some of the things I miss about her—her contagious laugh, her sharp wit and sense of humor, and so much more. It was a painful remembrance, and I could feel myself spiraling into discouragement. It was then I realized that I had a choice. I could let my thinking be caught up on the loss of those things or be captivated by the enjoyment of their memory. I chose the latter, and in the joy of those memories, my hope was elevated.

There is a law of physics that states that no two things can occupy the same space at the same time. This being true, what things are you allowing to occupy your thinking space?

I'm sure you've heard someone say, I can't stop thinking about... Actually, that is not accurate. You can stop thinking about one thing by exchanging it for another. You can lay down thoughts that are robbing your joy and your hope and pick up thoughts that generate the expectation of good. Unhealthy, dishonorable, or discouraging thoughts can be pushed out of your thinking by thoughts that are excellent and worthy of praise.

Exchange is a big part of living in the Kingdom of God. The composer Darrell Evans says it well. *I'm trading my sorrows. I'm trading my shame. I'm laying them down for the joy of the Lord. I'm trading my sickness. I'm trading my pain. I'm laying them down for the joy of the Lord.*[1]

What thought do you want to trade in for a better one? Think about it.

Never underestimate the power of a thought to feed your hope. You are not a victim of your thoughts, but you have the power to choose the ones you allow to color your internal world. This is not mind over matter but bringing our thinking into alignment with Holy Spirit, Who always has hopeful thoughts.

(1) Darrell Evans, 1998 Integrity's Hosanna! Music

Activation:

1. Set an alarm today to remind you every hour to think about what you are thinking about. Keep a journal.
2. At the end of the day, have a conversation with Holy Spirit about any exchange you would like to make.

Meditation:

II Corinthians 10:4-5

I Timothy 4:15

Joshua 1:8

Prayer:

Dear Father,

thank you for the grace to direct my thoughts so that I live in the hope you have given me. I declare that I am not a victim but a victor, and that by partnering with Holy Spirit, I will set my mind on that which is good and praiseworthy.

Journal

Ephesians 4:29

Let everything you say be good and helpful, so that your words will be an encouragement to those who hear them.

nlt

Day 10

Hope's Encouragement

There I was, standing on the platform of The Mission announcing the pregnancy of my daughter, Amy. It was a miracle! No, not my standing on the platform, but that a child was forming in my daughter's womb. The doctors had said there was no hope of her ever-having children, but Amy and Bryant's faith had remained strong through countless times of being prayed for. And now that which she had hoped for had become a reality.

Many of those sitting in the sanctuary that day understood the importance of the announcement. They had been praying for Amy for many years and realized that the impossible had become possible and a current reality. Rejoicing and celebration broke out in the room as they shared in our family's joy. But more than happiness filled the room.

There were those in that room that had come close to giving up, but when they heard the testimony, they began to believe again. People with long-term situations that never seemed to change suddenly were hopeful. The prophetic words that were almost forgotten took on fresh consideration. Through a word of encouragement, hope was released into the room, and those who had stopped believing for their own miracles became captivated with the expectation of good.

As prisoners of hope, we are always looking to build up and strengthen our own level of hope and for ways to promote the same in others. Encouragement is a powerful agent for both.

There are several ways we can encourage hope in ourselves and in others today. The testimony of God's provision is one of my favorites.

David understood the power of encouraging his hope through a testimony and we see it demonstrated when he volunteers to face Goliath. His brothers and King Saul viewed David's offer as one with no hope of success. David, however, encouraged himself through the testimony of his past history in God and pulled hope into his present, impossible situation.

Your servant has killed both lion and bear; and this uncircumcised Philistine will be like one of them... The Lord, who delivered me from the paw of the lion and from the paw of the bear, He will deliver me from the hand of this Philistine. I Samuel 17:36-37,

Not only did David's testimony breed hope and encourage his own heart, it did something to create hope in King Saul. Saul went from *You are not able to go against this Philistine,* to releasing the future of the army of Israel into the hands a shepherd boy: *Go, and the Lord be with you.* I Samuel 17:33,37

Positive, God-and people-honoring conversation is another way of encouraging our hope and the hope of others today.

What we say to ourselves and to others has great potential for good or harm. That's' why Paul tells us to Let everything you say be good and helpful. We have the power to create the world around us through the words we speak. It will either be a world that ignites hope or one that lowers the thermostat of expectation.

My granddaughter was ten years old when I was preparing to make a trip into the underground church in China. It was my first trip into that country and the fear of the unknown was draining my hope of successful ministry Samantha evidently had heard me express my concern and just prior to my departure, she handed me a handwritten note that remains in my travel bag to this day. I write it here as she wrote it, including the misspellings: *Throw an iron fist at the face of feer and evryware els the devil appears.*—Samantha Crone"

That word of encouragement written by my granddaughter on a scrap of yellow paper strengthened my hope and stirred my faith.

Deborah and I spoke at a women's conference in Sydney, Australia, several years ago. After the ministry time in one of the sessions, a woman came to me and placed a US penny on my palm and said unquestionably, *Here, this belongs to you. I found it on the floor.*

There was no uncertainty in the woman's voice or doubt in her words. She knew it belonged to me because I was the only one in the church that morning outside of Deborah that carried United States currency. I was identified by the currency I carried.

Encouragement is like that coin; it is one of the most recognizable currencies in the kingdom of God. As prisoners of hope, we have the privilege of being identified as people of the kingdom by the currency of encouragement.

Encouragement is also the primary language of the Holy Spirit. Paul writes in Romans chapter eight that the primary message of Holy

Spirit to us is that we are children of God. Let's not forget that Holy Spirit is the one that ramps up the level of our hope, ...that you may abound in hope by the power of the Holy Spirit. Romans 15:3. When we pay attention to His encouragement spoken into our spirit, hope grows from little to abundance.

When we speak a word of encouragement to others, we come into agreement with the character and message of the Holy Spirit. We participate in the very nature and ministry of the Spirit of God, and we are authentic expressions of the One who lives in us.

Fellow prisoner of hope, listen for and receive the encouragement God will be sending your way today. Don't reject or trivialize it. Embrace it, and let it do its work in you. Then keep your spiritual eyes open for the opportunities He will give you to spend the currency of encouragement on others.

Activation:

1. Set an alarm today to remind you every hour to think about what you are thinking about. Keep a journal.
2. At the end of the day, have a conversation with Holy Spirit about any exchange you would like to make.

Meditation:

II Corinthians 10:4-5

I Timothy 4:15

Joshua 1:8

Prayer:

Father,

thank you for the grace to direct my thoughts so that I live in the hope you have given me. I declare that I am not a victim but a victor, and that by partnering with Holy Spirit, I will set my mind on that which is good and praiseworthy.

Journal

I Samuel 17:36

Your servant has killed both lion and bear; and this uncircumcised Philistine will be like one of them...

nkjv

Day 11

Hope's Recall

The story of David and Goliath is more than the battle between a shepherd boy with a sling and a giant with a spear. In its detail, it gives us a key to living in an ever-growing and abundant hope.

When David arrived on the battle scene, the army of Israel had faced and failed against Goliath twice a day for forty days. Twice a day. That's at least seventy-eight times of running away in fear that fed their hopelessness. I think you can imagine the heavy sense of defeat that permeated the atmosphere throughout the camp as David approached his brothers with a few cheese sandwiches.

It didn't help David's confidence as he watched the armies of Israel march out in battle array only to see them flee the field as the giant moved toward them. David easily could have yielded to the dread-filled and demoralized condition of the army and returned home. Instead, he responded in hope, drew on his history, and took on the giant.

Let no one be frozen with fear because of Goliath David confidently declared *Your servant will go and fight with this Philistine.* 1 Samuel 17:31-37

When challenged in his ability to be successful against Goliath by King Saul, David told a story that gave the key to his hope of victory (paraphrased):

I may only be a keeper of my father's sheep, David began, *but when a bear or a lion came and took a sheep from the flock, I ran after it and hit it with my rod and took the sheep out of its mouth. When it turned to harm me, I grabbed it with my hands and killed it.*

David concluded his narrative with this statement, *I have killed both lion and bear, and what happened then will happen now. This uncircumcised Philistine will fall because he has defied the armies of the living God.*

This was not the statement of an arrogant young boy but the declaration of a developing king. David understood the power of linking his history in God to the challenge of the moment in order to feed his hope and act in courage.

This is critical for those of us choosing to live in hope. Without drawing on our personal history in God, our understanding of God's character and nature is relegated to the arena of theory and cold theological concepts. If we fail to connect our personal history with God to the beliefs we have of who God is, hope will fade as we are assaulted with contrary circumstances. This makes us vulnerable to lies about God and His faithfulness to us.

When Israel stood on the edge of the Promised land, facing all the challenges the land presented, they were armed with recent powerful experiences with God. These included being set free from slavery in Egypt, given a dry path across the Red Sea, and food being delivered every morning just to name a few. When Joshua and Caleb argued for going into the land, I believe they drew on those experiences and with confidence declared, *The Lord is with us*. Numbers 14:9

Yet the rest of the spies and all the people failed to connect their history in God with their present opportunity; and instead of professing hope, they made a hopeless declaration, *Because God hates us, he has brought us out of the land of Egypt...to destroy us* Duet. 1:27. Their failure to connect what God had done with what they now needed Him to do led an entire nation into forty years of wandering in the wilderness and the death of an entire generation.

Here is some good news for us today: When we take what we know the scripture says about God and connect it with our personal history with Him and bring that into our present situation, hope erupts and is nurtured. We then can confidently declare, *If God did it once, He can and will do it again.*

For me, God is good because as we buried our daughter, His presence sustained us, kept us, comforted us, held us, and gave us joy in a joyless circumstance. So now in every crisis or loss, I can draw on that history and hope is nurtured.

Jehovah Jirah is more than a name for God but a personal promise that God will provide. Why? Because the Bible says He is my provider, and I have personal history that I can draw on in every provisional challenge. Just one example of many: I can connect Jehovah Jirah with my experience of seeing God provide $400,000 for our church in one day then pull that encounter into the battle with any financial giant that stands in the way.

Having experienced that miracle of God's provision, I live with the expectation that when faced with a financial need, doubt and fear will bow and hope will soar. The expectation of good has become my default.

You say, *I don't have a personal history with God in that arena*. Then I suggest you get one. Take what it says in scripture about Him and believe it enough to test it. Put His promises up against the giant that stands in your way. Then the next time you face an obstacle you can say with confidence: *If God did it then, He can and will do it again*.

A friend of mine once said, *A man with an experience is never at the mercy of a man with an argument.* A person that has experienced the goodness of God will never bow to the accusations of the cynic or the lies of an enemy. Set your heart today to build a history with God that will stand as a bridge to hope.

Activation:

1. Ask Holy Spirit to remind you of a time in the past where God showed Himself faithful and powerful in an area you now struggling in. Journal it.
2. Write, draw, or create some other tangible reminder of that past experience and put it somewhere where it will serve as a regular reminder that you can connect between God's past and present faithfulness to you.
3. If you can't think of a past experience, find a scripture or a testimony that you can do the same activity with, and ask Holy Spirit to give you your own testimony in this area.

Meditation:

Psalms 34:8

Nehemiah 4:14

Prayer:

Thank you Father that you have given yourself to your people so we can know who you are and experience your love and goodness. Thank you that you give us evidence of your faithfulness and patience every day. I give you permission to expose me to encounters with you that open my life to greater understanding and revelation to live by.

Journal

I Timothy 1:18

This charge I commit to you, son Timothy, according to the prophecies previously made concerning you. That by them you may wage the good warfare.

nkjv

Day 12

Hope's Word

The prophetic words spoken over our lives are intended to declare who we are, remind us of our destiny, give us a glimpse of where we are going, and keep us in hope for the future fulfillment of all of that. In doing so, our prophetic words are weapons for the battle over hope.

Hope for our future, our dreams, and the completion of our assignments are always under assault from negative circumstances, the passing of time, the voice of the critic, and even the thoughts of our own mind. There isn't a day that our hope isn't confronted by at least one of these. With this being true, it would be wise for us to gain the full benefit of our prophetic words and use them as a weapon to strengthen our hope and fight off its enemies.

Getting all the benefit of a prophecy is not gained by static acceptance and off-handed treatment of the word. I can remember hearing teaching in the church years ago that we should place prophecies on the shelf; and if they are from God, they will come to pass. This laissez –faire attitude is simply a way to remove ourselves from the responsibility of partnering with God for the territory the Lord is offering us.

What we don't fully embrace, we trivialize; and what we trivialize, we never fully possess. Prophetic words require active hearing with a believing ear, judging with a discerning mind, believing it as God's word to us and our territory to possess, declaring it with a voice of faith, and activating the action points found in the word. When failing to fully embrace a well-judged prophetic word, we feed the enemies of unbelief, laziness, and indecision.

When we actively participate in prophetic words over our lives, they can then be used to fight off the forces of doubt and hopelessness. We can draw on their value and deposit them into our hope account

At the encouragement of the Lord, we had started a building project and determined that we would wait to draw the plans only when we had one million dollars in the bank. After over a year of raising the funds we had a total of only $120,000. At the prompting of the Holy Spirit, we gave all of it away to the Dream Center in Los Angeles.

Around that time, I awoke early one morning and heard a prophetic word directly from the voice of the Holy Spirit: *In one year you will have enough to start the building.* I knew that if I embraced that *one-year* word it would require that I declare it to the congregation. I have to admit that I didn't have the courage and didn't fully embrace the word. I wouldn't even tell Deborah about it.

A week later on an early Sunday morning, I had a vision of two events involving Deborah. During the Sunday service that morning, the vision came to pass in great detail. As I traveled home later in the day, I was curious as to what it all meant. Then the Holy Spirit broke through my thoughts and said, *I gave you that vision this morning and brought it to pass so that you would know that what I told you last week is the truth.*

I then had a choice to make—believe the word, declare it to the people, and live like it was true, or give up on the project. I chose to believe it and fully embrace it. In one year, we miraculously had the one million dollars in the bank.

That word of the Lord, along with the prophetic word of several well-respected prophets, and many scriptures the Lord had given us in the journey held us in hope during the many months of challenging circumstance.

On one such occasion when we were $1.5 million short of enough money to finish the building, those prophetic words became a powerful weapon. Deborah, my son Jeremy, and I entered the building one night, stood on the stacks of sheetrock, and declared all the prophecies and scripture we had been given. The next morning a man gave us $800,000, and shortly afterward on a Sunday morning, the people gave the remaining $400.000.

Recently, Deborah and I were traveling with some friends, and we were chatting about our prophetic promises. I noticed that we were often using the phrase, *If the word is true then...* We would then go on to talk about taking appropriate action. I had a sudden revelation that our words were betraying the desire of our heart to treat our words with complete faith. The word *If* was a subtle confession of doubt that revealed a hidden fear.

I said to my friend, *I think we need to change our language to fit what we believe. We don't take action on the word 'if the word is true' but 'because the word is true'.* Even as I was speaking, I could almost hear the *amen* of heaven and a greater sense of hope enter the car.

Prisoners of hope, don't let the enemies of unbelief, laziness, or indecision rob you of the value of your God-given words of promise. Today, pull out those promises that have come through prophetic words spoken to you, words that have come in your quiet time with the Lord and Scriptures that have inspired and captivated you.

Let's turn our, *If it's true* into *because it's true*, making those words powerful weapons of our warfare against the enemies of our hope.

Activation:

1. Find a written or recorded prophetic word that you received that is powerful and full of promise for you. Read and/or listen to it at least three times today. Allow yourself to believe the word and draw strength from it. Whenever the truth of this word is threatened today, declare aloud, *Because this word is true...* and speak to the truth of God's promise. If you have never received a prophetic word that you're aware of, ask Holy Spirit to give you one either directly from Him or through another person. Record and/or write it down when it comes.
2. Write down any scriptures or prophetic signs that God has been highlighting repeatedly for you recently. Take some time to stop and consider these, discern their source, and ask Holy Spirit to reveal anything He has been trying to tell you that you haven't taken hold of yet.

Meditation:

Numbers 23:19

Prayer:

Thank you Father for speaking destiny and hope through the gift of prophecy and the words of scripture. Holy Spirit, give me discernment and understanding to know the words I am to fully embrace today and the faith to act on them.

Journal

Proverbs 4:23

Keep your heart with all diligence, for out of it
spring the issues of life.

nkjv

Day 13

Hope's Heart

O ur heart is the place from which all life flows and the quality of our life is determined by the health of our heart. Since out of the heart flow all the issues of life, it's clear that our hope and our heart are intimately connected. This makes our heart extremely valuable and needful of protection, especially for those of us living in the expectation of good.

As prisoners of hope, we are as Solomon instructs us to *Keep our heart with all diligence.* To *keep* is to watch, guard, preserve, and protect. To keep the heart with *all diligence* is to keep it, keep keeping it, and never stop keeping it. It is to protect it as a most valued treasure. The New Living Testament translation of this verse states it this way, *Guard your heart above all else, for it determines the course of your life.*

If you were the parent of an eight-month-old child, and I were to ask you to take that child out onto the streets of your city and hand that child into the care of the first stranger you meet, you would believe me to be crazy. You would be revolted by the request and angry that I would even suggest it. No parent reading this devotional would follow my instruction, for that child is a valued and priceless possession. You would not trust that child to most of the people you know, let alone the stranger on the street.

Yet I find it interesting that many of us allow people we know, even strangers to possess our heart by giving them permission to plant destructive seeds of doubt, impurity, and negativity without any resistance. We leave our heart unprotected and susceptible to the diseases of the heart. Then we wonder why we are wrestling with bitterness, fear, offense, or hopelessness. The problem is that we have failed to keep our heart with all diligence, failed to guard it above all else.

In Proverbs 24:30-34, Solomon uses the field and vineyard as metaphors for the heart and makes the following observation,

I went by the field of the lazy man, and by the vineyard of the man devoid of understanding, and there it was, all overgrown with thorns. Its surface was covered with nettles; its stone wall was broken down.

As he continues to contemplate the condition of the field, he recognizes the cause, *A little sleep, a little slumber, a little folding of the hands to rest.* Through a lack of care and diligence, weed seeds had been allowed to find root, and the walls that were to keep out the predators had deteriorated, exposing the fruit of the vines to the little foxes.

Being willing to take a look at our field is essential for a healthy heart and life. I came across the following quote that speaks to the importance of noticing one's condition:

The range of what we think and do is limited by what we fail to notice. And because we fail to notice that we fail to notice, there is

little we can do to change—until we notice how failing to notice shapes our thought and deeds. R.D. Laing

A caution here is important. Honest self-awareness is an important part of keeping our heart healthy as long as the investigation is in partnership with the Holy Spirit. Deep navel-gazing will lead us on a path to condemnation and shame. The Holy Spirit, however, knows how to move us into loving repentance and joyful transformation as we journey with him.

Solomon doesn't stop with a simple though profound observation, and neither should we. Solomon makes two important statements: *When I saw it, I considered it well; I looked on it and received instruction* (24:32). Allow me to paraphrase this passage for understanding:

I walked by the field and there it was—being destroyed by weeds and predators. I paid attention to its condition and came to understand that it was the result of a lack of stewardship. The lesson was not lost on me, and I took appropriate action.

A good question to ask would be: what was Solomon's appropriate action? I'm confident that it was to keep his heart with all diligence.

There is an old English word that comes from the ancient warrior culture of English history that gives us a good picture of what Solomon is saying. It is the word *fealty.* When a king would raise up an army in order to expand or defend his territory, he would require his soldiers to pledge their allegiance to him and his kingdom. This aligning of loyalty was known as *swearing fealty.*

To swear fealty was to relegate oneself to faithfulness and fidelity in the service of the king—even to the sacrifice of one's own life.

Upon swearing fealty, the warrior and all his resources, were now committed to serve and protect the king and his kingdom. This is what it means to keep our heart with all diligence—to pledge allegiance to the health and welfare of our heart, to devote all our resources to serve and protect the most valuable part of us—the place where all the issues of life, including our hope, are nurtured.

As a prisoner of hope, let this day find you living in covenant with your heart, keeping it with all diligence.

Activation:

1. Write out a covenant promise to guard your heart.
2. Memorize it and speak it out loud at least seven times during your day as a declaration of your pledged fealty.
3. Ask Holy Spirit to partner with you in the diligent guarding of your heart and listen for His instruction.

Meditation:

Matthew 5:8

Luke 6:43-45

Psalms 19:14

Prayer:

Father,

Thank you for reminding me of the value of my heart and the importance of guarding it every day. I look to you, Holy Spirit, to be my guide in this journey. Where there are seeds of doubt, fear, bitterness, or hopelessness, weed them out by your love and hope. I give you permission to keep me weed free! I open my heart to everything you have for me and ask for discernment in all areas of my life.

Journal

Proverbs 13:12

Hope deferred makes the heart sick, but when the desire comes it is a tree of life.

nkjv

Day 14

Hope's Antidote

elayed is a word the frequent flyer rarely, if ever, welcomes—especially when attached to the flight home. I love being with our friends in the nations and sharing life and ministry in other cultures. But when it's time to go home, I'm like a racehorse heading for the barn and delay is not my friend.

Delay can be a nagging enemy of hope, constantly declaring that what you are expecting will never come to pass. However, here is the good news for all prisoners of hope: Hope is the enemy of hope's enemy. Sound like double talk? Then let me say it this way: Hope is the antidote to the hopelessness of delay.

Solomon the wise, makes an intriguing statement when he writes, *Hope differed makes the heart sick, but when the desire comes, it is a tree of life* Proverbs 13:12. When there is a prolonged delay in the coming of the thing we are hoping for, our heart can come under attack and be susceptible to the diseases of the heart: brokenness, disappointment, disillusionment, and bitterness among others.

We have all grown weary in the waiting. In those times when it seems nothing is happening or moving forward, we are tempted to dwell on fruitless questions. Will the promise ever come true? Why is this taking so long? You may be in this place today and it feels like the delay is killing you!

So, what's the answer to the enemy of delay? There is a key hiding in plain view within Solomon's instructions: Don't defer your hope! Don't put off or abandon your expectation of good. Without hope, there is no hope so keep living in the expectation of the fulfillment of the desire and the tree of life that it will produce. Choosing hope is the antidote for the heart diseases to which delay makes our heart vulnerable.

Hope is made for the time of delay, the times when evidence of the promise hides and the thing hoped for seems impossible. These are the times hope shines the best and stands in the face of delay and declares, *You'll not defeat me—not on this day!* Hope is not a thin strand of thread we cling to, but it is a stronghold that surrounds us and holds us secure in the time of delay.

Simeon, a man spoken of in Luke's gospel, had a promise from God that he would live to see the Messiah in his lifetime. The scripture doesn't tell us how long Simeon had been waiting, how long it had been from the hearing of the promise to the day he walked into the Temple and saw Jesus in the arms of Mary and Joseph. Luke simply states *it had been revealed to him by the Holy Spirit that he would not see death before he had seen the Lord's Christ.* Luke 2:26

What we do know from Luke's account is that Simeon was prepared for the moment the prophetic word was fulfilled. By remaining hopeful, he stayed sensitive to the voice of the Holy Spirit and did not allow delay to dampen his expectation. When he heard the instruction of the Holy Spirit to go into the temple, he responded and his prophetic word became a reality.

Just like Simeon, you may have some prophetic promises that you are waiting to see become reality. The good news is that just like Simeon, when you choose to live in hope in the time of delay, the discouragement of delay is defeated. You are then available to cooperate with the timing of God and prepared to take hold of the promised result when it comes. As a prisoner of hope, you have permission to make time pay for your advancement and require delay to further your dreams.

The process of time is necessary for the completion of promises in our lives. That process is more than just allowing time to pass. Time itself does not heal all wounds and neither does it on its own bring all things to pass. Standing in hope turns the process of time from an enemy to a friend and allows us an opportunity to cooperate with the Holy Spirit and position ourselves to receive the promise.

Activation:

1. Make a list of all the ways you can turn delay into valuable preparation. When you run out of ideas, ask Holy Spirit to give you a few more. Implement at least one idea on the list today.
2. Write down 3-5 things that the Lord has promised you, which have not yet come to fruition. Spend some time thanking Him in advance for their eventual fulfillment.
3. Spend a couple minutes in partnership with Holy Spirit, considering the condition of your heart. Has it become sick or hardened through delay? If so, ask the Lord to heal your heart and renew your hope.

Meditation:

Luke 2:25-35

I Samuel 1-20

Prayer:

Dear Father,

I set my heart to hope in you today in the face of delay's accusations, so that my life will cooperate with your process. Thank you for caring enough for me to allow time to become my friend and hope to be my constant companion, reminding me of the inevitable fulfillment of your promises.

Journal

Matthew 5:13-14

You are the salt of the earth...You are the light of the world.

nkjv

Day 15

Hope's Influence

L ife around us is a blank canvas on which we can paint a picture of hope, using the brush of influence.

Have you noticed when reading the gospels that people enjoyed being around Jesus? Everywhere He went crowds gathered, the influential sought Him out, and even the unwelcomed of society hosted Him in their homes. Jesus was a person of influence. So are you and I.

Influence is the capacity of persons or things to be a compelling force on, or produce effects on the actions, behavior, opinions, etc., of others.[1] Simply stated, influence is the effect we have on the people and atmosphere around us. The good news is that we have the power to choose the texture and impact of that affect.

Jesus said we are salt and light, both powerful influencers. He doesn't instruct us to become either of these elements, but simply declares that we are. The issue Jesus was addressing was not one of working at becoming but one of embracing and releasing what we have become.

Believers should be the most sought after employees and the best employers in the city. We should be known for our integrity, character, honesty, wisdom, and creativity. It should be said of us that our influence has made the world we work in a better place.

Whenever we host conferences, I remind the attendees to make sure and be generous to the wait staff in the restaurants in our city. We want the waiters and waitresses to look forward to the times the Christians sit at their table.

I love the song written by Bryan and Katie Torwalt, *When You Walk into the Room*. It's a beautiful expression of the influence Jesus has wherever He goes. Below are some of the stanzas from that song:

"When you walk into the room, everything changes; darkness starts to tremble at the light that you bring.
"When you walk into the room, sickness starts to vanish; every hopeless situation ceases to exist."
"When you walk into the room, the dead begin to rise, 'cause there is resurrection life in all you do."

I awoke one morning singing this song and enjoying the sense of peace and hope that its words and melody inspires. I then heard the Holy Spirit say, *This is what I want to be said about my people. When my people walk into the room, everything changes, darkness trembles, sickness vanishes, and hopeless situations cease to exist.* I was immediately impacted by the deep cry of the Father's heart for His children to be transformational and the promise of His presence that was implicit in His words.

When we walk into a room, we carry our influence with us. If people in that room know we are coming, our influence precedes us, is effective while we are there, and lingers when we leave. We carry with us an influence that will shape the atmosphere of that room. Our presence can produce any number of results—it can inspire or bore, increase hope or promote despair, give comfort or raise anxiety. We determine what that result will be by choosing what we allow to influence us.

The story in Acts 5 of the people bringing the sick and laying them out on the streets so they could receive healing from the shadow of Peter is a powerful reminder that what influences us will influence the world around us. Peter carried on the inside a presence that spilled out onto the street and people were healed.

Jesus gave us a picture of the conduit of hope our lives can be to the hope-seeking world around us when He declared:

He who believes in Me... out of his heart will flow rivers of living water. But this He spoke concerning the Spirit, whom those believing in Him would receive. John 7:38-39

Jesus is speaking of rivers flowing, not ponds stagnating. We have been filled to spill—not a little, but with an atmosphere-changing, world-transforming deluge of life. Notice, Jesus states *rivers* not *a river*. I believe one of those rivers of life that flows from the Holy Spirit through our lives and into our arenas of influence is hope.

I would suggest that as prisoners of hope, desiring to influence the world around us for good that we make the bridge of the Torwalt's song our prayer today:

Come and consume, God, all we are. We give you permission; our hearts are yours, we want you, we want you.

(1) Dictionary.com

Activation:

1. Write down the people who have had the most influence in your life, past and present. Thank God for any positive influence they have made and ask Holy Spirit to displace any negatives in favor of hope.
2. Write down the names of three people in whose lives you know you have influence. Spend the day praying for them and asking Holy Spirit how you can better partner with Him in encouraging hope in their lives.

Meditation:

Luke 19:1-10

Acts 5:14-16

Prayer:

Father,

thank you for the world you have placed me in and for giving me your Spirit. Thank you that you have made me salt and light so that I can influence the people in my life for your kingdom. I give you permission, and I open my heart up to be continually being filled with your life-giving water. Fill me with courage to be what you have made me to be and carry out my assignment as a prisoner and carrier of hope.

Journal

Matthew 5:16

Let your light so shine before men, that they may see your good works and glorify your Father in heaven

nkjv

Day 16

Hope's Simplicity

As I approached the checkout counter of the grocery store to have my groceries priced and bagged, the young woman behind the counter averted my gaze, mumbled some sort of practiced greeting. Her body language told me she was enduring her work day and expected nothing pleasant or encouraging from the people she was serving. She wasn't rude; she just exhibited a practiced and protective aloofness.

Hello, Sandy, how are you today? I had never met Sandy, but I assumed she was Sandy because her name tag indicted it to be true.

Sandy looked up from her task with a startled expression and noticed that I was looking her in the eye, smiling and awaiting her response. Her delayed reply of *I'm good, how are you?* demonstrated a much more friendly and engaging manner.

I'm good, too. How is your day going? I again inquired.

Her response this time was more revealing and warm, and her countenance had significantly brightened. As she continued to ring up my purchases, our conversation became an increasingly pleasant experience, and I left her smiling and inviting me to return soon.

Deborah and I have made a practice of engaging in these kinds of encounters. We look for opportunities with grocery clerks, sales people, hotel personnel, janitorial staff, coffee shop baristas, airport porters and security personnel, airplane stewards, restaurant wait staff—just about anyone who is serving us. The reaction is almost always the same—a brightened countenance, a pleasant response, and often a self-revealing that surprises us. Many of these opportunities open the door for us to pray with or prophesy over the individual.

These experiences cause me to wonder how seldom that grocery store clerk, hotel bellman, or janitor is treated like a real person by the people they are serving. How many people checked out at their counter, rode with them in an elevator, took a Grande latte from their hand, and never noticed them or asked their name, let alone spoke a pleasant word. How many days had they faithfully done their job while unthinking and sometimes unkind customers reinforced their sense of a lack of value. How many Christians, who carry the light of the most encouraging and hope-generating being in the universe, failed to take the opportunity to make that person's day?

It also made me wonder, could it be that letting our light shine is just as simple as a courteous act of kindness? Is it possible that looking someone in the eye, giving them a smile, and speaking a kind word is actually a more effective distributor of hope than we think?

Let's be reminded that kindness is a fruit of the Spirit that lives in us. The fruit of kindness like the other fruit of the Spirit is to be enjoyed by the people around us. It may be good for us to check today on the fruit that people are exposed to from our life. Is it bitter or sweet; are we offering the fruit of the flesh or fruit of the Spirit?

Let's also remember that it is the Lord's kindness that brings people into a journey of reformation. Here is Paul's word on the subject:

Are you unmindful or actually ignorant of the fact that God's kindness is intended to lead you to repent—to change your mind and inner man to accept God's will? Romans 2:4, Amplified Bible

We are carriers of hope, and our hope is not just about us. As we explored on day 15 of this journey, we are to be influencers in our world, distributing hope as salt that flavors and light that illuminates and warms. We are to be a flowing river of life not a dead sea.

Here's the good news: Kindness is a powerful way to open the heart of a person and dispense hope—hope to believe for forgiveness, hope to believe for salvation, hope to believe there is something better, hope to have faith for breakthrough, hope to believe someone cares, and hope to believe in the one who is able to do exceedingly, abundantly, above all we can ask or think.

Again, it's not complicated. It can even be done anonymously.

Several years ago, Deborah started doing an anonymous random act of kindness for young parents. As she walks down the grocery aisle where the baby food is stocked she will remove a jar and put a dollar bill, sometimes a five-dollar bill, in the space and replace the jar. As she prays for the right person to pull out that jar, she imagines the reaction of that parent when he or she sees the gift.

There's no telling what joy and hope will be sparked through that small gift in the heart of that mom or dad.

As carriers of hope, let's look for opportunities to be kind today; they are invitations from the Spirit for us to be like our Father.

Activation:

1. Write about a time that someone went out of his or her way to express kindness to you, noting how it made you feel and the effect that it had on you. Let that memory inspire you, and ask Holy Spirit to highlight an opportunity for you to similarly impact someone else this week.
2. Spend an entire week challenging yourself to always look every person you interact with in the eye. If possible, use their name at least once and give them a smile or a compliment. Be intentional to create a *splash zone* of hope and kindness around you.

Meditation:

Luke 10:30-37

Prayer:

Father,

I thank you that for your kindness shown to me when I deserved none. I desire to be like you in demonstrating this fruit of your Spirit to the people around me. Holy Spirit, guide me into full fruit so that everywhere I go Jesus will be glorified and recognized.

Journal

Proverbs 18:21

Death and life are in the power of the tongue, and those who love it will eat its fruit.

nkjv

Day 17

Hope's Speech

Solomon, known for his wisdom, puts language to what we experience every day in our world of words: *Death and life are in the power of the tongue.*

It is not a new revelation to any of us that words have power. Words have the power to build up or tear down. They create atmosphere and increase or release tension. We all have experienced the sensation of the air being suddenly sucked out of a room when someone makes a statement that everyone is thinking, but no one else has the courage to speak.

We live in a world of words that have influence on our thoughts and impact on our actions. As Solomon states, we eat of the fruit of those words. Most of us carry words in our memory that were spoken to us sometime in our history. Some of those words created life, and some released death. When remembered, they still produce emotions tied to the nature of the words. No matter how long ago the words were spoken, they cause joy or sadness, laughter or tears. Words have the power to leave a lasting mark on us.

Words have the power to strengthen determination, release courage, and unleash hope. They also can deflate resolve, create confusion, and produce discouragement. The power of the tongue is in the words it forms and that power for life or death cannot be understated.

Ideologies, concepts, and strategies all find power in the language used to describe them. Words bring life-altering thoughts out into the open where they manifest their intent. An idea partnered with language is like the two parts of a compound being joined together to form a powerful chemical reaction.

The High Priest and the Jewish Sanhedrin of the first century understood well the potential of language partnered with truth. Having arrested the apostles Peter and John for proclaiming the resurrection of Jesus, their solution to keep the message of the man Jesus from spreading was to command them to stop speaking about Him:

So they summoned them and imperatively instructed them not to converse in any way or teach at all in or about the name of Jesus. Acts 4:18, Amplified Version

Later, after they were released and had gathered with other believers, the apostles prayed a prayer that reflected their understanding of the importance of words:

Now, Lord, consider their threats and enable your servants to speak your word with great boldness. Acts 4:29, NIV

Abraham Herschel, a Polish-born American rabbi and author, has been identified as the author of the phrase, *Words create worlds*. As if to illustrate the thought, those three words create for us a world of limitless possibilities. Herschel along with Solomon (whose words Herschel has simply restated) is giving permission to choose the world we create—one of life or one of death, one of hope or one of hopelessness.

So, prisoner of hope, what do all these words about words have to do with hope today? Simply this—hope is often word-activated. We have the power to create a world of hope for others, as well as ourselves, by the words that we speak.

What kind of world do you want to live in? Have you ever listened to your own words? Since we hear our own words, it might be good for us to pay attention to the expressions that come out of our mouth. After all, we are surrounding ourselves and those around us with the world our language is creating. What, we must also ask, does the world look like being created around the ones who are hearing our conversation?

These questions should not be condemning or embarrassing questions to prisoners of hope. Rather, they should inspire and challenge us to create a world filled with the expectation of good. It is our privilege to be world changers and atmosphere transformers by the words we speak. With a simple conversation saturated with hope we can make an eternal difference.

I awoke one Sunday morning with the heaviness stemming from the opposition the church was experiencing and feeling like the man who told his mom, I don't want to go to church this morning. Those people don't like me and I'm not sure I like them. His mom responded, But son, you have to go, you're the pastor!

I crawled out of bed, went to my computer, and pulled up my sermon for the morning. As it was loading, I decided to check my emails and there found eight words that held a life-giving message of hope that gave a much-needed expectation to my world. The email was from a young man in the church, directed by the Holy Spirit to send me a hope hand-grenade. The words that landed on me and exploded in hope that morning was this simple: *I am proud that you are my pastor.*

Jesus said, *Out of the fullness—the overflow, the superabundance of the heart the mouth speaks* (Matthew 12:34b, Amplified Version). So, here, fellow prisoners of hope, is our challenge: To be hope speakers, we must have a hope-filled heart.

How do we do that? We can start this journey by praying the prayer of David: *Let the words of my mouth and the meditation of my heart be acceptable in your sight, oh Lord, my strength and my redeemer.* Psalms 19:15

I then suggest that we surround ourselves with words, conversations, declarations, meditations, and testimonies saturated and infused with hope. Most of all, let's hang out with the God of hope and go on an adventure with the Holy Spirit, the one who causes our hope to abound.

Activation:

1. Are there any words spoken by yourself or others that have been tormenting you? If so, choose to forgive the speaker of those words and offer their painful memory to the Holy Spirit. Ask Him for healing and redeeming words to create a new, hope-filled memory in that area of your life.
2. Offer your conversation to Holy Spirit today as an offering, and ask Him to give you words of life and hope to speak in every situation. Think of an area where you need hope, and speak words of life into that same area of another person's life today; sometimes there is great power in giving others the encouragement that we need ourselves.

Meditation:

Isaiah 50:4-5   Proverbs 10:19-21   James 3:1-13

Prayer:

Holy Spirit,

thank you that you have chosen to live in me. I welcome your instruction and count on your wisdom. Cause my heart to overflow and abound with hope and my words to be filled with the expectation of good. Guard my heart and my mouth that in all things I may please you.

Journal

Matthew 6:22

The lamp of the body is the eye. If therefore your eye is good, your whole body will be full of light.

nkjv

Day 18

Hope's Lens

The servant of Elisha could not believe his masters response to his cry for help. The story, told in the sixth chapter of the book of II King registers the servant's cry and the master's reply (paraphrased):

What are we going to do? the servant cried out in fear. *The army of Syria is surrounding the city and I don't think this is a good sign!* Elisha's response was one of fearless confidence, *Don't worry about it, there are more that are for us than those who are against us.*

These two men, the servant and his master, were seeing two different realities because they were looking through two different lenses. When God opened the servant's eyes, giving him a new lens, the servant could then see that the mountain was full of horses and chariots of fire. The servant was able to see what had been hidden from his natural eyesight.

Life is full of many kinds of surprises, experiences, and circumstances. Some are enjoyable and some not so much. Personal crises, financial pressure, employment anxiety, the challenge of change—both good and bad—all are part of life on this planet. There is no telling what kind of surprises are waiting for you today.

The lens through which we see the things of life determines our perception and understanding of what life is to us. Our perception then forms the perspective that becomes our reality. That reality may or may not be accurate and certainly not complete, but it will influence the level of our hope.

Here is today's good news: The quality of the lens will determine the accuracy of our perspective, and as prisoners of hope, we can choose the lens.

Moses was carrying the weight of leading a nation through a very difficult transition from bondage to freedom, from a slave culture to a military force. He knew a battle was on the horizon and was wearied by the stubbornness of the people. When we pick up the story in the thirty third chapter of Exodus, Moses has just made the most important decision of his life:

If your presence does not go with us, do not bring us up from here. Exodus 33:14,

The Lord responds positively to Moses, agreeing to go with them into the land:

I will also do this thing that you have spoken; for you have found grace in my sight, and I know you by name. Exodus 33:16,

It is then that Moses, believing he has permission and favor, asks God for the thing he knew would be important for the tasks ahead:

And he said, 'Please, show me your glory.' Exodus 33:18,

It is in that moment that Moses learns the defining quality of the glory of God: goodness.

The he said, 'I will make all my goodness pass before you.' Exodus 33:19,

I believe that Moses understood the enormity of the task before him. He knew that moving the people into the promised land was going to be difficult and he would need a lens through which to view all that was going to be thrown at him. God revealed his goodness to give Moses perspective.

We talk often about the goodness of God and rightly so. He is supremely good. In fact, his goodness is so intensely good that God could not give Moses a full dose. And though it may take eternity for us to grab hold of the full revelation of God's goodness—for every aspect of the character and nature of God is an eternal adventure—I am confident that a revelation of His goodness is the lens that allows us to live in hope.

I love Maui Jim sunglasses. They were one of the first sunglasses made with lenses that allow you to see what is otherwise hidden from your natural eyes. I learned how useful they were on a trip to the home of their creation, Maui.

On a beautiful, clear Hawaiian day, Deborah and I were out sailing on a catamaran and watching for humpback whales. When spotted, the captain would slow the boat to a stop and we would wait for the whales to breach. On one such occasion, one of the crew excitedly cried, *There it is, just under the water right next to the boat.* This was what we were all waiting for. I moved with everyone else to her side of the boat and excitedly looked down into the water. My enthusiasm deflated when all I saw were steaks of sunlight on blue ocean.

Everyone else was oohing and ahhing while I was feeling left out. At first, I thought it might have something to do with my color blindness, so I asked Deborah to help me by pointing out exactly where the whale was and what to look for. Still, I could not locate the humpback that everyone else was enjoying.

It was then I realized that I had my Maui Jims positioned on the top of my head and not on my face. When I placed the sunglasses over my eyes, the glare from the sun on the water disappeared and the whale lying just under the surface appeared. I needed the right lens in order to see past the glare and find what was hidden under the water.

The lens of God's goodness allows us to see through the glare of the stuff of life and see the hope God hides in every situation. Prisoner of hope, you have been given like Moses permission and favor to ask for a fresh revelation of God's goodness. Put on your spiritual Maui Jim sunglasses of His goodness and see what is hidden for you to find.

Activation:

1. Ask Holy Spirit to remove the glare so you can see clearly where to look for His blessing, hidden in any discouraging or overwhelming situation you face today. Whether you immediately see it differently or not, thank Him for His goodness and the help of His presence.
2. Ask Holy Spirit to bring to your memory a time when you were particularly affected by the glare of life's circumstances. Ask Him to help you look again at those circumstances through the lens of His goodness and let Him minister to your memories through that perspective.

Meditation:

I Corinthians 6-12   Psalms 31:19

Psalms 27:13   Psalms 33:5   Psalms 107

Prayer:

Father,

I declare that you are good and that there are hidden promises of hope in everything I will go through today. Grant by your Spirit a greater revelation of your goodness. I desire your goodness to overwhelm me, take me by surprise, and open my eyes to all you have planned for me. I will worship you and not withhold my praise, giving thanks continually for your goodness.

Journal

Romans 8:31

What then shall we say to these things? If God is for us, who can be against us?

nkjv

Day 19

Hope's Reason

What is there to be hopeful about today? Good question, prisoner of hope. We could search and find some positive events or situations to focus on, and I encourage that we do so. We could make declarations that are in the opposite spirit from some of the negative circumstances that we face today, and again, I encourage this proactive way of putting our mind into the context of hope.

However, I believe the answer to what there is to be hopeful about today is best addressed by the words inspired by the Spirit of God Himself and recorded by the Apostle Paul in Romans chapter eight.

We probably all agree that though there are many parts of the Bible that speak of love, I Corinthians 13 is best known as the love chapter. In that chapter, Paul lays out for us the supreme importance of love and the definitive description of what love looks like.

I would propose that though hope is a theme throughout scripture that Romans 8 is the hope chapter or at least one of the great ones. Paul, describing all the works of God on our behalf and the resulting benefits, gives a compelling argument for embracing hope every day of our lives. The following is a brief synopsis of the case for hope found in Paul's letter to the Romans.

Paul begins the chapter by declaring that we who have been made free from the law are no longer living under the condemning nature of the law and free to live according to the Spirit. This has been made possible by the work of Jesus Christ on the cross. He affirms that we are living with the Spirit of God alive in us. He is the same Spirit that had the power to raise Jesus from the dead and, therefore, gives resurrection life to us. I'm thinking this is good news and reason to hope.

Then Paul continues to give us encouragement as he declares that we are not slaves or orphans but are fully adopted children of God that have been invited into an intimate father/child relationship. This relationship guarantees our inheritance and dispels all fear and is the primary message of the Holy Spirit in us. He is the same Holy Spirit that intercedes on our behalf, being strong for us in our weakness. All of this, too, seems to be news that gives strong evidence to bolster our claim to hope.

Now we come to an unreasonable reason for hope: God has committed himself and all his resources to guarantee that everything that we go through in life—the good, the bad, and the ugly—will be made to benefit us in our journey. Not only that, but He determined a long time ago that we were going to be successful in our journey into being like Jesus. I get the feeling that when God sets His will to something, it is as good as done. Don't you agree that hope continues to win the argument?

Paul goes on to state that you and I have been called and glorified: Called by our name to bear His name; and glorified—made worthy of one to be boasted of.

So, with all that Paul writes being true, he now poses the crux of the argument for living in hope: *What shall we say about such wonderful things as these? If God is for us, who can ever be against us?* 8:31, NLT This is a mic-drop moment. If God is for us—which is rhetorical by the way—can there be any doubt as to the ultimate outcome of this day?

Let's review the things that God has done that have bearing on our hope today:

- He has set us free from the condemnation of the law and has given us the liberty of living in the Spirit with resurrection power working in us.
- He has adopted us with all the rights and privilege of a first-born son. In doing so He gives us our true identity.
- He has guaranteed to turn all the experiences of life in our favor and determined long ago that we will be like His Son.
- He has given us His name and is proud to boast of us as His children.
- He is for us and not against us, securing our victory.

It would seem that the question for hope in this day is well answered, yet Paul lays down a further argument to bolster His conclusions in verses 32-37. Let me put it in my own words:

Why would the God who gave His Son for us hold back anything that is good for us? If God has called us innocent, who can make an accusation against us or condemn us for the failures of who we used to be? On top of all that—who can separate us from the love of the

God that is for us and not against us and has made us excel in victory?

Paul's final declaration capsulizes the answer to the question: What is there to be hopeful about today? Here it is from the Mirror Bible:

This is my conviction, no threat whether it be in death or life; be it angelic beings, demon powers or political principalities, nothing known to us at this time, or even in the unknown future; no dimension of any calculation in time or space, nor any device yet to be invented, has what it takes to separate us from the love of God demonstrated in Christ. Jesus is our ultimate authority. Romans 8:38-39

Prisoner of hope, what is there to be hopeful about today? In Christ Jesus—everything!

Activation:

1. Make a list of reasons that God has given you to hope in Him. If you can't think of anything, ask the Holy Spirit for inspiration. If you still can't think of anything, rewrite the bullet point list in this chapter using your own words. Thank God for what He shows you and let it fill you with hope!
2. Write a brief declaration from your list that you can memorize and speak out loud several times today.

Meditation:

Romans 8

Psalms 23

Psalms 124

Prayer:

Thank you Father for all you have done on behalf of your children. Thank you that I stand today secure in your love and free from the condemnation of my past and can live with confidence as your child. As I face this day with all its challenges, I declare that in you I have reason to be a prisoner of hope and can expect your good in all things today.

Journal

Hebrews 3:6

And we are his house, if indeed we hold firmly to
our confidence and the hope in which we glory.

niv

Day 20

Hope's Confidence

*P*risoner of hope, it is time to come out of hiding and live boldly in the hope that is yours as a child of God, Today, celebrate your coming out party

The author of Hebrews 3:6 uses one of my favorite words in the New Testament. In its Greek form, *paresis* is most often translated *boldness* or *confidence* and the most common definition of *paresis* is, *free and fearless confidence, cheerful courage, boldness, assurance.* [1] It is, however, a multi-faceted word that has some interesting dynamics. Each one gives us useful insight into living in bold, confident hope. The following are two of those helpful dynamics.

Paresis is to live *openly, frankly, without concealment.*[1] In other words, to be bold or confident is to walk through our physical world and live in the kingdom of God without timidity, acting as if we belong. We have been given a place on this globe by virtue of our physical birth, and a purpose in the kingdom of God by virtue of being born again. We belong here, and if we are to live in full expectation of good, we must live boldly, not allowing fear to diminish our hope.

Paresis additionally is the *deportment by which one becomes conspicuous and secures publicity.*[1] I can best illustrate this dimension by speaking of my grandson, Nolan Ryan Crone. Nolan is five years old and does not quietly or unnoticeably enter a room. He explodes into the room, and everyone knows he has arrived and that he has a purpose in being there. He certainly knows how to be conspicuous and secure publicity.

I am not proposing that we are to be obnoxious or brash, but as prisoners of hope, we are here in this world to make a difference, and to intentionally bring hope to hopeless people. This requires confidence that shouts with the voice of hope: *Tada! A prisoner of hope is here!*

Yet another definition of *paresis* is to be *without ambiguity or circumlocution* [1] These are big words with important meaning. To live with confidence as carriers of hope is to be clear in our purpose, without doubt about our foundation and straightforward in communicating the reason for our hope.

The powerful nature of this word *paresis* can be seen in the following passages of scripture.

In Hebrews 3:6, the reader is encouraged to hold firmly to, or keep secure possession of, our confidence and hope. In so doing, the writer validates the importance of both our confidence and our hope. I believe, the one is strongly connected to the other. I propose that hope empowers confidence, and confidence is required for the acting out of our hope. *And we are his house, if indeed we hold firmly to our **confidence** and the **hope** in which we glory.* Hebrews 3:6, NIV

In another passage in the same book, the writer of Hebrews speaks of the necessity for boldness when entering the throne of grace if we have any hope of securing grace or mercy: *Let us therefore (because we have a high priest that understands us—see verse 15) come **boldly** to the throne of grace, that we may obtain mercy and find grace to help in time of need.* Hebrews 4:16

In his first instructive letter to believers, the apostle John writes about the privilege we have to come and ask anything of God and then receive what we ask. He states that our expectation to receive from God is in our confidence that we are asking according to His will. *Now this is the **confidence** that we have in Him, that if we ask anything according to His will, He hears us. And if we know that He hears us, whatever we ask, we know that we have the petitions that we have asked of Him.* I John 5:14-15

The apostle Paul writes in his second letter to the Corinthian Christians that our hope, found in a greater, superior new covenant, empowers our boldness. *Therefore, since we have such a **hope**, we are very **bold**.* II Corinthians 3:12, NIV

Again we go to the writer of Hebrews for insight. *Therefore do not cast away your **confidence**, which has great reward.* Hebrews 10:35 This verse, followed by the next four verses, gives us an understanding of the importance and imperative of living with *perisis*. I offer my amplified version of these verses based on word study and context.

Do not throw away or lose by default your free and fearless assurance, which of its own is of great benefit. For through your tenacious determination to not give up on what God has promised, to keep hoping in spite of circumstance, you will receive your promise.

For there is a time delay between the promise and its fulfillment, creating pressure to draw back and give up territory that has been

designated for you. It is territory that is your inheritance; it belongs to you, and it is the Father's good pleasure to give it to you. By giving up hope, you rob the Father of His pleasure in seeing you possess what is yours.

However, that will not happen. We will not cower under the pressure and yield territory that belongs to us. We are those who live in hope and walk in faith, taking hold of all that has been given to us and becoming all we have been created to be.

As prisoners of hope, we leave our homes and enter the world with a confident expectation that shouts to all we come in contact with, *I'm a carrier of hope, and that hope is chasing you down!*

(1) Blue Letter Bible Lexicon for Hebrews 3:6. www.Blue Letter Bible.org

Activation:

1. Using scripture and prophetic words you have received, write a declaration of who God says you are. Declare it aloud until you're able to say it with boldness and confidence. It isn't arrogance to agree with what the Father says! Stand with your hands on your hips and face set confidently forward in the so-called "Superman" pose while you make your declarations. Standing in this or another confident posture for a sustained time has been scientifically proven to boost confidence.
2. Set a timer on your phone to remind you every hour today to stop and meditate on the declaration you wrote. Meditate on the truth and significance of these things, and thank God that you have confidence in knowing He loves you and lives in you.

Meditation:

Hebrews 10:19-25; 35-39   Romans 5:1-5

Prayer:

Father,

thank you for hope that stands strong in every part of life. Thank you that you have given me every reason to be confident in hope no matter what else is going on in my life today. I set my heart and my mind to live boldly and assertively as a prisoner of hope.

Journal

Romans 4:18

Against all hope, Abraham in hope believed and so became the father of many nations, just as it had been said of him, 'So shall your offspring be.'

nkjv

Day 21

Hope's Risk

Hope should always take us into faith—for hope is the father of faith. It was while living in the hope of a son that Abraham believed. In hope, he had faith to believe for the completion of the promise that he would be the father of a nation.

Hope is essential for the sustaining of faith, for it is the expectation of good that feeds the level of risk that faith requires. Faith is the outworking of hope and the evidence that proves we have been living in hope.

Now faith is the confidence in (resolution regarding) *what we hope for and assurance* (proof, conviction) *about what we do not see (what we are hoping for).* Hebrews 11:1, NIV, emphasis mine.

By faith, Noah built an ark because he had hope of being rescued. He risked rejection, his reputation, his resources, even his family to act on the hope promised by God. If Noah had never hoped, he would not have had faith to build a boat that would save him and his family.

By faith Gideon gathered with 300 men and took on the army of over 135,000 men, horses, and chariots with a torch, a horn, and a vase. He risked his life and his nation because he had hope in the power of God to bring victory. Hope for a better future placed in the God of promise caused him to risk it all in faith.

Abraham took the son of his promise to an altar at the instruction of God. It was by faith that he offered his son; and the writer of Hebrews reveals that he did so because he hoped in God, concluding that even if Isaac died, God would raise him from the dead.

By faith, Moses gave up the riches and comfort of Egypt for the wilderness, putting at risk his future because he had hope of something better: *He thought it was better to suffer for the sake of Christ than to own the treasures of Egypt, for he was looking ahead to his great reward.* Hebrews 11:26, NLT

Faith is not faith without a response. Behind every act of faith is the partner and foundation of hope.

Faith, which is hope acted on, is risky because by its very nature it is putting something at risk. Hope, like faith also requires a measure of risk. The very act of hoping is to risk unmet expectations. Since what we are hoping for has not yet appeared we risk failure and the loss of what we hoped for.

I lived a large part of my life in the prison of fear of failure. I was unwilling to put my reputation at risk so I would limit my opportunities to advance at the level I felt comfortable and secure. I have come to believe that a hesitancy to embrace hope, fueled by the fear of unmet expectations held my faith captive.

It wasn't until I ventured to dream—to hope for something that captivated my heart—did faith begin to grow. When I dared to hope, the fear of failure bowed to the altar of the possibilities faith offered. The risk of failing and losing my reputation was no longer my master. I moved from being a captive of fear to a prisoner of hope.

There are several questions I often ask myself in order to test my risk level. Here are a few:

- Have I become satisfied with security and become averse to being uncomfortable?
- Has the calculator of human reasoning started dictating my faith?
- Have I become more concerned about what I have to lose rather than dreaming about what I have to gain?
- Has anything become so valuable to me that it overshadows my value for the manifest presence of God?
- Are there places in my journey where I am standing in the boat waiting for the waves to calm down while Jesus is saying *come?*
- What choice am I making every day to stay where I am rather than putting my comfort at risk in order to find that next place that God has for me?
- Am I still a dreamer, or am I content with memories?
- Have I stopped hoping in God for the greater glory?
- Is my heart still set on an adventure in God?

My list may not be yours, but I suggest you create your own check list that challenges you to stay a prisoner of hope and move in faith. It will be risky, but the good news is we are held secure in the hands of one who is never going to let us go.

On our 25th wedding anniversary, Deborah and I celebrated by spending a few days in beautiful Victoria, British Columbia. The day we arrived I spotted a 1958 Vintage Beaver pontoon plane tied to the dock. In my world, flying in a plane about the size of a Volkswagen was a perfectly good way to celebrate our anniversary.

I proposed it to Deborah, and much to my surprise, she agreed—though a bit reluctantly.

I jumped in next to the pilot and Deborah took the seat behind me and we lifted off and headed over the island. Soon the plane began to respond to a great deal of turbulence. Deb was starting to get a bit nervous, and I was even wondering if this was such a good idea when the pilot's voice came through our headphones. *Are you guys alright with this?* Deb's response again surprised me as she boldly replied, *I'm alright if you're alright.*

Prisoner of hope, we were made to live in hope and fly in faith. Let's not be afraid; we are alright if He's alright, and believe me—He is more than alright.

Activation:

1. Create a list of questions for you to check what level of hope and risk you are living in. Put a reminder in your phone or calendar to monitor your progress.
2. Journal about some promises God has made you or risks He has called you to take that you have been avoiding or delaying. Ask God for courage and strategize with Holy Spirit about how you can refresh your hope and what steps you can take this to move toward those promises and callings.
3. Ask Holy Spirit to show you if there are any specific fears that are stealing the hope needed to act *in faith. If so, declare aloud, I renounce the fear of _____ ! I break all ties with it and put myself back under the authority of the God of hope today.*

Meditation:

Hebrews 11

Prayer:

Thank you Father that I am secure in your hands. Grant me courage today to risk in hope and faith what is temporary in order to win that which is eternal. I choose to adventure with you as a prisoner of hope.

Journal

Other Books by David Crone

Heroes of Hope

Heroes of Hope is a collection of inspirational stories of either historical or Biblical characters who have lived with hope in challenging times. In doing so, they have inspired hope in the people around then and made significant contribution to their world and future generations.

Heroes of Hope is a companion book to *Prisoners of Hope* and *21 Days of Hope*.

PRISONER OF HOPE
FOREWORD BY KRIS VALLOTTON

In Prisoner of Hope David Crone lays out a powerful argument for the importance of choosing hope and living with a confident expectation of the goodness of God. David speaks from life experiences that have challenged the validity of a hopeful existence and reveals the keys to defeating those negative circumstances. Prisoner of Hope is not a book of theory or cold theology, but a breathing epistle of the authentic value of living in expectation. In reading this book you will re-discover your childlike faith and your heart will be freshly tuned to the life giving sound of hope.

DECLARATIONS THAT EMPOWER US
FOREWORD BY KRIS VALLOTTON

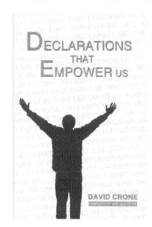

Declarations That Empower Us is a training manual for anyone wanting to partner with heaven for personal or corporate breakthrough. These declarations are dedicated to transforming our minds so that we can view life through God's eternal perspectives, and bring hope to this desperate and dying planet. Every Christian needs to read this book! Without question, this book will change your thinking and transform the world around you. Some of the declarations in this book are already bringing life and hope to individuals and church communities in many places throughout the United States and in several countries.

DECISIONS THAT DEFINE US
FOREWORD BY BILL JOHNSON

The message that will change the world is only as strong as the transformation that has first taken place within believers. In Decisions that Define Us, David Crone documents his personal and corporate journey of transformation as senior leader of a transitioning church in Northern California. Each decision in this book represents the spoils of a battle fought and costly kingdom lesson learned by this leader, his team, and their local fellowship. Within these pages you will be challenged and inspired to pursue God's Kingdom at any cost and to discover practical ways of expressing the supernatural in your own life.

THE POWER OF YOUR LIFE MESSAGE
FOREWORD BY BILL JOHNSON

Author David Crone shares his deeply personal journey experiences that ended with an intimate relationship with His heavenly Father. You will be challenge to change your mindset, which opens the door to internal transformation. You will learn how to define your life message and how to make decisions that lead to fulfilling God's exhilarating and exciting plans for your current and eternal destiny.

Books can be purchased at www.imissionchurch.com or www.amazon.com

About the Author

David Crone and his wife, Deborah, are the Senior Leaders of a community of believers called The Mission in Vacaville, California. They have been in full-time vocational ministry for over 45 years and have served at The Mission for over 25 years. While at The Mission, they helped transition a local church into a global ministry that provides resources for their region and the nations. Their value for team ministry has developed a culture of strong leaders, some of who serve with David and Deborah on the core leadership team of The Mission. Their lives and ministry are known for authenticity, a passion for God's presence, and a pursuit of His kingdom on Earth.

David is a director of the Mission School of Supernatural, a ministry of The Mission, and, along with Deborah, serves on the teaching staff of the school. In partnership with The Mission, NIS Ventures, and Kingdom Development Group of Australia, David has developed supernatural training schools in the Philippines and Fiji. He serves as the International Director of Mission Fiji and Deeper Life, Philippines.

David and Deborah have traveled extensively, ministering in 23 nations. David is the author of five books. Deborah, an accomplished artist and designer works as the project Manager at The Mission, having overseen 100,000 square feet of building remodeling. David and Deborah are welcomed speakers at conferences and churches both at home and overseas.

Made in the USA
San Bernardino, CA
20 November 2017